Tips from the Quad

Other books in the Wisdom & Warnings® series

From Divorce Mess to Happiness

The Badass Woman

Let Them Fly

Because You Care

Happily Ever After

Our library of wisdom keeps growing!
Check out the full list anytime at wisdomandwarnings.com or
simply scan the QR code.

Tips from the Quad

*Your 365 Day Roadmap
to College Success*

Jen Fort

From the Wisdom & Warnings®
book series

Disclaimer

The author of *Tips from the Quad* is not a licensed therapist. Because of this, this book is presented solely for educational and entertainment purposes and is not intended to be a substitute for the advice of a physician, professional coach, therapist, and other qualified professionals.

This book was created with the assistance of various resources, including AI as a brainstorming tool to help organize ideas and enhance clarity. However, all insights, concepts, and creative content are entirely the author's.

Dedication

This book is dedicated to everyone eager for higher education, yet open to learning from the practical experience of others.

I wish you a lifetime of curiosity, adventure, and fulfillment.

What People Are Saying

"I remember feeling bittersweet and carrying my memories of high school close to my heart, but my college years were the first launching point for me to find my independence and begin to make sense of the world. Of course, college also included some of the most difficult challenges I'd faced at that point in my life. The first steps toward independence and adulthood are both terrifying and exhilarating.

The book you're about to read not only shares valuable wisdom and insight that can help you navigate this journey, but it also confronts the difficult realities of this transition in life. At this moment of writing, it's been eight years since I graduated, and a lot of these life lessons in this book have helped me in my life outside of college just as much during.

One of the nuggets of wisdom that resonated with me most, however, was, "Even if you never fully understand your role, trust that your presence and efforts are shaping the lives of those around you in ways that you may never fully see" (pg. 138).

So, as you embark on this new journey, remember that you are the one who forges your path in life. In those moments when nothing makes sense, when your role feels insignificant, know that you will shape the lives of other people around you in ways that you could never imagine. It is now your time to step out into the world and shout with enthusiasm, 'Here I am.' "

-Mark Nyman

"Learning how to ask my parents politely step back and let me grow up was a game-changer. We're in a really good place now."

— *Jessica W., Penn State University*

"I didn't realize you could change academic advisors! I wish I had known that earlier."

— *Mark M., Penn State University, PA*

"I had so many issues with my roommate. Hopefully, by sharing my story, someone else can do better."

— *Stephen M., Penn State University, PA*

"I learned really fast going home those first few weekends was a mistake. I wish someone had encouraged me to stick around; it would have made my freshman year so much easier."

— *Morgan O, West Chester University, PA*

"Never to surprise your parents with a new tattoo."

— *Rob W., Kutztown University, PA*

Share Your Wisdom!

Wisdom & Warnings consists of nearly 8,000 carefully curated nuggets of wisdom on dozens of topics related to life's milestones, ranging from relationships to parents/children to education and career, plus fun topics for living your best life.

Engage with the Wisdom & Warnings community for ongoing encouragement through life's milestones.

www.wisdomandwarnings.com
Facebook: https://www.facebook.com/wisdomandwarnings/
Instagram: @wisdomandwarnings
Email: hello@wisdomandwarnings.com

Table of Contents

My Story

There's something magical about hearing the right words at just the right time—a spark of wisdom that can brighten a day, guide a decision, or even change the course of a life. I've always been drawn to those small but powerful truths. From an early age, I found myself captivated by people's stories—their struggles, triumphs, and the nuggets of wisdom they carried. Every person I met seemed to have something unique to teach me, and I couldn't help but ask: *What's your lesson?*

That curiosity became the seed of a passion I call *Wisdom & Warnings*—a lifelong quest to learn from the experiences of others. Over the years, I turned conversations into a collection of insights. Friends, family, and even strangers shared their advice with me, often without realizing how profound their words were. By the time I looked back, I had gathered over 8,000 pieces of advice—a treasure chest of wisdom just waiting to be shared. But for the longest time, I didn't.

Self-doubt became my shadow. *What if I fail? What if no one cares?* Those questions kept me in a cycle of "someday" and "not yet." I tinkered with the idea for over a decade, hesitating to commit fully. Deep down, though, I couldn't shake the feeling that this treasure wasn't meant to stay hidden. Whenever I thought about shelving the project, a little voice whispered, "Life is too short not to learn from each other." It felt selfish not sharing, but fear has a way of making even the best ideas feel impossible.

*Fear, my friends, is a topic for another time.

Then, life gave me an unexpected push. I lost my job—a moment that felt devastating at first but turned out to be the break I needed. Suddenly, I had time to reflect, and one thing became crystal clear: it was now or never. Those whispers urging me to share my collection became impossible to ignore. I realized that I didn't need to be perfect or polished; I just needed to start.

So, I took a leap of faith with no formal writing experience and zero understanding of the publishing world. That leap became the *365 Days of Wisdom & Warnings* book series. Along the way, I've made mistakes, learned lessons, and celebrated every small victory. More than anything, I've realized that when you listen to the quiet whispers of your heart, you're led to something greater than fear: purpose.

If this journey has taught me anything, it's that the world needs what only you can offer. You might feel unqualified or unsure, but someone out there is waiting for what you have to give. My wish for you is this: trust those quiet whispers, silence the doubts—whether they're yours or someone else's—and chase what sets your soul on fire. Your passion could be the light that sparks someone else's journey. And isn't that the real magic?

I'll be cheering you on.

Jen

Introduction

First, congratulations! You're about to start one of your most exciting and life-changing chapters. College is an amazing opportunity, but let's be real: it's perfectly normal to feel nervous or overwhelmed right now.

Even those who seem to have it all together feel apprehensive when heading to college. From new classes to new friends and figuring out how to live on your own—there's a lot to juggle. And honestly, there will be moments when it seems too much, and you might want to quit.

That's where this book comes in. It's filled with tips from real people—students just like you, parents, and even college grads—who've already been there, screwed up, and learned some hard lessons. The tips and advice inside this book come from their experiences, mistakes, and things they wished they knew before they started.

This book reminds you that it's okay not to have it all together. You'll face challenges and make mistakes, and that's all part of the experience. The tips in this book will give you a head start, some insider knowledge, and a little extra confidence to take on whatever comes your way.

So, take a deep breath, get excited about what's ahead, and trust that you've got this. A whole new world is waiting for you at college—one where you can grow, thrive, and make the most of the lessons shared by those who've been there before.

Welcome to your next chapter. Let's get started!

Chapter 1

The Final Countdown: What to Do Before Leaving for College

Day 1

---

*The months before you start college will be stressful,
and everyone will be on edge.*

The months leading up to college can feel like a rollercoaster, and it's not just you who's feeling the pressure—everyone around you will be on edge. Your parents might be fussing over everything, and your friends might be acting weird because they're stressed, too. You might feel pressure to get everything perfect, but don't let it get to you. Take a step back when things start to feel overwhelming and remember that this is a significant change for everyone. Focus on what you can control, like packing, getting your paperwork sorted, and catching up with friends. If things get heated with your family or friends, try to stay calm—everyone's dealing with worries in their own way. The stress will pass, and soon, you'll start a new adventure.

Day 2

Grab the earliest move-in time slot you can.

Getting the earliest move-in time slot is a game-changer! You avoid the chaos of packed hallways and elevators later in the day and get first dibs on the best spots for unpacking and organizing your stuff. With fewer people around, everything feels less rushed, and you can take your time setting up your dorm how you like it. Plus, getting there early gives you a chance to meet your RA, scope out the vibe of the building, and even connect with a neighbor before things get hectic.

Day 3

Plan your move-in with military precision!

A little strategy goes a long way on move-in day. Start by assigning specific tasks to everyone who is helping you. One person does a quick cleaning, someone else takes charge of furniture assembly, and someone else acts as the "runner" to pick up pre-ordered items from local stores. Be super strategic about how you pack and unpack. Remove items from their original packaging beforehand to save time and reduce clutter. Having a clear plan and everyone working efficiently will make your move-in process smooth and stress-free and set you up for success in your new space.

Day 4

The more underwear you take, the less often you need to do laundry.

Your schedule will be packed, and laundry won't be at the top of your to-do list. Trust me; you'll thank yourself for having spare pairs when you're too busy studying or hanging out to worry about clean clothes. Laundry days can get pushed back when you've got more important things going on, and having enough underwear gives you that extra cushion. Plus, doing laundry in college can be a hassle—you might have to wait for machines or pay for each load, so it's not something you'll want to do every few days.

Day 5

Packing will be tricky if you're going to school in a different climate.

Start by researching the weather patterns for the school year and pack strategically for each season. If you're moving somewhere colder, invest in a good-quality winter coat, waterproof boots, and plenty of layers. Focus on breathable fabrics, sunscreen, and comfortable shoes for warmer climates. You don't need your entire wardrobe immediately—you can always add pieces as the seasons change, and buying from local stores ensures they have the right clothing for their specific climate.

Day 6

Prepared to feel overwhelmed.

Starting college can feel like a crazy mix of excitement and chaos. Feeling overwhelmed is normal—you're not the only one. You'll be meeting tons of new people, adjusting to a different schedule, and dealing with schoolwork, all while figuring out who you are and where you fit in. The trick is to accept those feelings and cut yourself some slack. Break things down into smaller tasks, figure out what needs to get done first, and handle one thing at a time. Just take a deep breath and embrace the messiness.

Day 7

Learn to complete your own FAFSA form.

If you've never completed a FAFSA form, don't stress—it's not as complicated as it looks. Grab your social security number, tax info, and any other documents they request, and dive in. Completing the form yourself helps you understand how financial aid works, which will come in handy later. Knowing where your money comes from and what's expected of you will help you make smarter decisions. Take it one step at a time, and don't rush, but still pay close attention to deadlines. If you get stuck, you can call many online resources and even a helpline. You might even call 1-800-MOM-HELP (just joking; this is <u>not</u> an actual phone number).

Day 8

Get a passport.

Whether it's a last-minute chance to travel internationally over spring break or an unexpected study abroad opportunity, having a valid passport means you can say yes without any hassle. Getting a passport can take up to two months, so it's wise to get it sorted out now rather than waiting until you need it in a hurry. If you already have a passport, make sure it has at least two to four blank pages and renew it at least six months before it expires to avoid any last-minute issues. Having it ready means you'll never have to turn down an adventure because of paperwork.

Day 9

Don't skimp on computer maintenance.

Keeping your computer in good shape is essential for college success. Regularly back up your files to an external drive or cloud storage to protect your work in case of technical issues. This simple habit can save you from losing important documents if your computer crashes or stops working unexpectedly. If your computer does break down, don't panic—fall back on old-fashioned pen and paper to keep up with notes and assignments until it's fixed.

Day 10

Set boundaries with parents for how often you'll call.

Although it might seem awkward, setting expectations is important so no one feels abandoned. Your parents will want to check in a lot at first because they care about you. But you'll also be busy settling into your new life, making friends, and managing your schedule. To avoid misunderstandings, honestly discuss how often you'll call or text. Maybe it's a quick text every other day or a call once a week—whatever works for you both. It's all about finding a balance that lets you maintain your independence while maintaining a strong family connection.

Day 11

What you do in college matters more than where you go.

Your success depends on how you make the most of your time, no matter where you go. What counts is getting involved, working hard in your classes, building relationships with professors and new friends, and seeking out opportunities that push you to grow. Whether at a big-name university or a smaller school, the key is to stay focused on your goals and take advantage of everything college offers. Join clubs, apply for internships, and don't be afraid to step out of your comfort zone. Most employers care more about your experience, skills, and achievements than the school you attended.

Day 12

No air conditioning? Accommodation might be available.

Check with your campus housing office to see if they offer any accommodations, like fans, air purifiers, or even the chance to move to a different room. Let them know about any specific health issues or allergies you have so they can help make your living situation more comfortable. It's better to address this early than wait until you're in a tough spot. Most schools want to ensure their students are comfortable and healthy, so don't hesitate to ask for what you need.

Day 13

Consider every possible source of financial aid.

Many lesser-known scholarships and grants could help ease your financial burden. Local organizations, businesses, and community groups offer scholarships, some based on hobbies, interests, or specific fields of study. Also, investigate state-specific aid, work-study programs, and internships that pay you while you learn. Even if you don't qualify, apply anyway—you'd be surprised how many funds go unused simply because people don't bother. The more creative and proactive you are when seeking these opportunities, the less likely you'll find yourself drowning in debt later.

Day 14

Set up a medical power of attorney.

A Medical Power of Attorney (POA) is a simple but crucial legal document that gives someone you trust—like your parents—the ability to act on your behalf if you're hospitalized and unable to communicate. College can come with surprises, from accidents to sudden illnesses, and having this in place ensures that someone is ready to advocate for you when it matters most. Talk to your parents about setting this up before you head off. It's not just about legalities; it's about peace of mind—for you and them.

Day 15

Live on campus for at least the first year.

Living on campus helps you immerse yourself fully in college life and makes it easier to meet new people. You'll be right in the middle of all the action, from study groups to campus events, and you won't have to worry about commuting or finding a place to park. Plus, living on campus gives you a chance to adjust to your new routine without the added stress of off-campus responsibilities like utilities or managing a lease. You'll also have access to campus resources, like libraries, fitness centers, and dining halls, which can make your life more convenient and help you stay focused on what truly matters... your education!

Day 16

Don't go home the first few weekends.

During the first few weeks, it might be tempting to escape to familiar surroundings, but staying on campus can help you adjust and make the most of your new environment. The first few weeks are crucial for settling in, meeting new people, and feeling at home in your new space. By sticking around, you'll participate in activities, join clubs, and meet new friends, making you feel more connected to campus life. It will feel even more uncomfortable if you come back from a home visit and it seems everyone but you have made new friends. Don't let that happen!

Day 17

Hold off on getting your books until after the first class.

College books can be super pricey, but you can save a lot by simply waiting. Hold off on buying any books until after your first class—professors often adjust the syllabus, and you might find out you don't need every book listed. Once you know exactly what's required, skip buying new whenever possible. Look for textbook rental sites, digital versions (which are often cheaper), or even free PDFs online. Ask your professors if older editions are acceptable, as they often cover the same material at a fraction of the cost. You can also check out textbook exchange programs or student buy/sell groups on social media to find used books at lower prices. By waiting and exploring these options, you'll avoid unnecessary purchases and keep more money in your pocket.

Day 18

Learn to take care of yourself when you're sick.

Start by keeping a basic health and first aid kit in your dorm with cold and flu medicine, pain relievers, and a thermometer. Remember to pack Band-Aids, antiseptic cream, and something else for muscle soreness. If you are sicker than a common cold, know where the campus health center is and how to make an appointment. It's also wise to plan for getting help if needed—know who to call or text for advice or just a bit of support. Practice self-care by getting enough rest, staying hydrated, and managing stress.

Day 19

It won't be easy; but it will be worth it.

College isn't always a walk in the park. You'll face challenges, late nights, and moments when you want to give up. But here's the deal: all those struggles are part of what makes the experience worth it. The hard work you put in, the obstacles you overcome, and the growth you achieve will pay off in ways you can't fully appreciate in the moment. Take failure, for example. Maybe you bomb a big exam after thinking you had it all figured out. In the moment, it feels like the end of the world. But later, you'll realize that experience taught you how to bounce back—how to study differently, ask for help, and not let one setback define you. It's not just about the grade; it's about building resilience that will carry you through life's bigger challenges.

Day 20

Go to all orientations.

It might sound boring or something you can skip, but attending orientations is worth it. These sessions are designed to help you get the lay of the land, meet people, and start feeling comfortable in your new environment. You'll learn about necessary resources, like where to get academic help, how to navigate campus, and what activities are available. Plus, orientations are one of the best ways to meet other new students who are in the same boat as you. Skipping out means missing valuable information that could make your transition smoother.

Day 21

Your parents will be nervous, and emotions may run high.

As you prepare to leave for college, remember that your parents probably feel a mix of pride, excitement, and nerves. They've spent years looking out for you, and now you're about to take a giant step toward independence. This can be a little scary for them, even if they don't show it. You might notice them being more protective or emotional than usual, or they might want to spend extra time with you before you go. Try to be patient and understand where they're coming from. Keep communication open—talk about your feelings and listen to their concerns. Let them know you appreciate all they've done to help you reach this point. A little extra understanding can go a long way in keeping things calm and positive.

Day 22

Pack your clothes for college, then take half.

You don't need as much as you think, and you'll want to save space for other important stuff. Dorm rooms are small, and you'll probably end up wearing the same favorite outfits over and over anyway. By keeping it simple you'll have less clutter and less laundry. However, don't hold back when it comes to underwear and socks—bring more than you think you'll need. You'll never regret having extra, especially during those busy weeks when laundry isn't happening. Think about what you wear and what you can mix and match for everything else.

Day 23

Honesty and a roommate agreement help prevent conflicts.

It might be tempting to downplay your habits to seem more laid-back and avoid potential conflict, but being upfront is key. If you're a neat freak, say so. If you like to stay up late, let your roommate know. The last thing you want is to live with someone whose habits clash with yours simply because you didn't speak up. Consider having a roommate agreement. While it might feel unnecessary when things are going well, it's really a tool to help prevent conflicts before they start. Think of it as a blueprint for living together—covering everything from cleaning responsibilities to quiet hours. You may not realize its value until a disagreement arises, and by then, having clear expectations already in place can make resolving issues much easier.

Day 24

Understand the basics of your medical insurance.

Sometimes, you need to find medical care off campus. Be prepared and figure out what your family's medical plan covers—like whether you need a referral to see a specialist or if there's a copay when you visit a doctor. Make sure you know where to go for medical care near your campus and whether those providers are in-network. If your insurance is through your parents, discuss what to do if you get sick or injured while away. It's one of those adulting things that might seem overwhelming at first, but having a grasp on it will make your life a lot easier when it counts.

Day 25

You don't need a printer, but having one in your room at 2 a.m. is convenient.

You can get by without a printer in your dorm room, but there's something to be said about having one right there when you need it, especially at 2 a.m. when a deadline is looming. Sure, the library or computer lab has printers, but they're not always open, and getting there might be a hassle in the middle of the night. Having a printer in your room is super convenient, especially when you're running on little sleep and need to get things done fast. You might not use it every day, but when you do, you'll be glad it's there.

TIP: Coordinate with your roommate so you don't end up with two.

Day 26

Taking a car to campus can be a real hassle.

Having a car seems like freedom but can quickly become a hassle. Parking on campus is usually a nightmare. Spots are limited, expensive, and often far from where you need to be. You'll also have to worry about keeping up with gas, maintenance, and potential parking tickets, which add up fast. Plus, having a car can make it easier to skip out on campus life and head home on weekends, which can keep you from fully diving into the college experience. Most campuses have pretty solid public transportation, and ride-sharing apps like Uber or Lyft are always available when you need to get somewhere off-campus. If you do take your car, never store valuables inside!

Day 27

Schedule ahead for doctor appointments for
breaks when you're home.

Call your doctor's office well in advance and set up appointments for winter and summer breaks. This way, you can secure an appointment and focus on relaxing and catching up with friends and family when you're home instead of trying to fit in a last-minute doctor's appointment. It's one less thing to worry about, and you'll feel good knowing you've got it all taken care of. Planning for this might not seem like a big deal, but it can make your college life much smoother and give you peace of mind.

Day 28

Take plenty of pictures but be choosy about what you post because pictures live online forever!

While it's great to document your life, be smart about what you post online. Once something's on the internet, it's out there forever, even if you delete it. Future employers, schools, and even people you haven't met could see what you post. Before you hit Share, think about how it might look to someone who doesn't know you well. A funny photo now might not seem so amusing years down the line when you're applying for a job or an internship. Also, remember that privacy settings can only do so much—screenshots and shares can spread things further than you'd expect.

Day 29

Take a small flashlight and plenty of batteries.

It may not seem like a big deal now, but when you find yourself in a dimly lit dorm room or the power goes out during a storm, you'll thank yourself for being prepared. Late-night fire drills or unexpected emergencies happen, and a reliable flashlight can help you from draining your phone's battery. Plus, a flashlight can offer extra peace of mind if you end up in an unfamiliar part of campus after dark. Throw it in your bag, stash it in your desk, or keep it by your bed—make sure it's easy to reach when needed.

Day 30

Fill prescriptions over the summer or during winter break.

The best time to refill your prescriptions is over the summer or during winter break when you're home and have easy access to your usual pharmacy. Do this at the doctor's appointment you booked in advance. This way, you can avoid the stress of finding a new pharmacy near campus or dealing with insurance issues when you're already busy with classes and adjusting to college life. Talk to your doctor about getting a larger supply, like a 90-day refill, so you don't have to worry about running out during the semester.

Day 31

Take a mini tool kit with the essentials.

Having a few essential tools on hand can save you many headaches. Whether it's hanging up pictures, tightening a loose screw on your chair, or even just opening a stubborn package, a mini tool kit will come in handy more often than you'd expect. Include things like a small hammer, straight and Phillip's head screwdrivers, pliers, Command adhesive strips, and a tape measure.

Day 32

Pack a spill-proof mug or two.

Having a spill-proof mug will save money and reduce waste by skipping disposable cups from the campus coffee shop. Here's a pro tip: choose an ugly one. If it's not the prettiest mug, you're less likely to misplace it or have someone else accidentally claim it as theirs. Ugly mugs have a way of sticking around. So, find yourself a sturdy, spill-proof mug, and let it become your trusty sidekick through all those early mornings and late-night study sessions.

Day 33

Learn how to manage stress productively.

Stress is going to happen—the trick is to find healthy ways to cope. Exercise is a great way to blow off steam, whether it's hitting the gym, going for a run, or even just taking a walk. Sometimes, stepping away from the books and getting some fresh air can do wonders to clear your mind. Another way to manage stress is by staying organized. Keep a planner or use a scheduling app to track assignments, deadlines, and other commitments so you don't feel overwhelmed. It's also important to make time for things you enjoy—whether it's a hobby, hanging out with friends, or just relaxing with a good movie. And never underestimate the power of a good night's rest.

Day 34

Under-the-bed storage bins can be a lifesaver!

Space is going to be tight, and you'll quickly realize that every inch counts, so making the most of the space under your bed is a smart move. Under-the-bed, bins are perfect for storing things like extra clothes, shoes, bedding, or even snacks—basically anything you want out of the way but still within easy reach. This way, your closet won't overflow, and your room won't look like a tornado hit. Plus, under-bed storage keeps everything dust-free and organized, so you don't have to dig through piles of stuff to find what you need.

Day 35

Learn to prepare your own taxes.

It might sound complicated, but getting the hang of it early can save you time and stress later. Start by understanding the basics, like what documents you need—W-2s if you have a job and any other income records. Many colleges offer resources or workshops on tax preparation for students. There are also plenty of online tools and software that simplify the process, guiding you step-by-step through filling out forms and claiming deductions. Even if you don't earn much, knowing how to file a simple return can be super helpful. It's also a good habit to track your annual expenses and income, making tax season less of a scramble. If you get stuck or have questions, don't hesitate to ask for help from family members, friends, or a tax professional. Getting comfortable with taxes now means you'll handle your finances more confidently in the future.

Day 36

Don't dwell on high school once you're in college.

Clinging to high school can keep you from fully experiencing everything college has to offer. You must be open to new friendships, challenges, and opportunities waiting for you. It's okay to remember the good times, but don't let them hold you back from making new ones. High school was just the beginning; college is where you start to grow into who you will be. Dive into this new chapter with an open mind. Get involved, explore new interests, and embrace the freedom and responsibility that come with being a college student. The more you focus on where you are now, the more you'll get out of the experience.

Day 37

Learn the difference between a big problem and a bad day.

Not everything that feels overwhelming is a crisis; understanding this can help you manage stress better. A big problem is something that genuinely affects your future or well-being, like serious personal issues. A bad day, on the other hand, might mean you spilled coffee on your shirt or a rough interaction with a roommate. While these things can be frustrating, they're often manageable and temporary. Learning to distinguish between the two helps you stay calm and focused. When you face a bad day, remind yourself that it's just one rough patch and won't define your whole college experience. For more complex problems, seek help from resources like advisors, counselors, or trusted friends.

Day 38

Learn basic self-defense.

College is an amazing place, but it's also a time when you'll be out on your own, maybe for the first time, and it's important to feel confident in your ability to protect yourself. Taking a self-defense class can teach you simple techniques to defend yourself if you ever find yourself in a sketchy situation. It's not about being paranoid—it's about being prepared and aware of your surroundings. Plus, self-defense isn't just about physical moves; it's also about learning to trust your instincts and making smart decisions. It might even make you feel more empowered in everyday situations, like walking home at night or navigating unfamiliar places.

Day 39

Credit cards are a slippery slope; choose wisely.

The temptation of a freebie might make a credit card seem like a great deal, but it's important to look beyond flashy promotions. Before applying, understand the terms and have a plan for managing your spending and payments. If you decide to get a credit card to build credit, choose wisely—student credit cards often offer lower fees, reasonable interest rates, and features designed to help you build credit responsibly. Look for cards with benefits that fit your needs, like no annual fees or spending trackers. Building good credit is important, but it's even more critical to do it wisely. Don't get swept up by quick rewards—focus on smart financial choices.

Day 40

Know how to kindly ask your parents to back off.

Your parents will be excited and a bit worried, which might lead them to be overly involved in your new life. When you need space, approach the conversation with understanding and respect. Start by acknowledging their support and how much you appreciate it. Then, gently explain that you're learning to handle things independently and need the chance to make your own decisions. Use "I" statements to avoid sounding accusatory. Here is a good example: "I feel like I need a bit more space to figure things out for myself." It's helpful to suggest specific ways they can support you, like having scheduled calls instead of constant check-ins. This way, you show that you're still open to their guidance but in a way that fits your new independence.

Day 41

If you vent to your parents when you're sad or frustrated, tell them when you feel better.

Parents want to be there for you but worry when they hear you're struggling. If you only share the tough times, they might always feel anxious or stressed about you. Keeping them updated when things improve shows them that you're handling situations and that you appreciate their support. A quick message or call to let them know you're okay can ease their worries and keep your relationship strong. Plus, sharing the ups and downs helps your parents feel involved in your life and strengthens your bond.

Day 42

Save important phone numbers to your phone.

Your insurance card is crucial for accessing off-campus healthcare services if you get sick or injured, so keep it handy. You never know when you might need it, whether for a check-up, an emergency or just dealing with health-related questions. Alongside your insurance card, jot down important phone numbers—like your insurance provider's contact number, primary care doctor's office, and any campus health services. Having these numbers readily available can save you time and stress when making quick calls or appointments. It might not be the most exciting thing to think about, but it's a practical step that can make a big difference in managing your well-being smoothly while you're away from home.

Day 43

Don't borrow money for daily expenses.

It's tempting to think of a quick loan or credit card as an easy fix for things like snacks, books, or small outings, but it can lead to stress and debt. Instead, create a budget that covers your needs and stick to it as closely as possible. This means planning for groceries, transportation, and other routine costs. If you are short on cash, look for ways to earn a bit extra, like a part-time job or freelance gig, rather than relying on borrowed money. Managing your finances responsibly now sets you up for better habits in the future and keeps you from accumulating debt that can be hard to manage.

Day 44

Get a flu shot as soon as it's offered.

College life means lots of people in close quarters, and that's a perfect setup for the flu to spread quickly. Getting your flu shot early helps protect you and those around you from getting sick. It's a simple step to save you from missing classes, feeling miserable, or dealing with health complications. Many colleges offer flu shots on campus, making it super convenient to get vaccinated.

Day 45

Learn how to handle conflict in person.

College life brings you close contact with all kinds of people, and conflicts can arise over anything from shared spaces to differing opinions. Instead of relying on text messages or social media to vent or resolve issues, practice addressing problems face-to-face. Direct communication helps you understand the other person's perspective and find a solution together. It's much easier to misinterpret messages online, and avoiding in-person conversations can lead to more significant misunderstandings. If you're nervous about this, start by having honest conversations with friends and family before you leave for college. Embrace face-to-face communication and make it a habit.

Tip: You can always ask for roommate mediation where the RA can help you both resolve the issue.

Day 46

Invest in good headphones, then don't lend them out.

Good headphones can make studying, relaxing, or hanging out much more enjoyable by blocking out distractions. You'll want to protect your investment since good quality headphones can be expensive. They might get damaged, lost, or not returned if you lend them out. Plus, do you want them to come back with someone else's earwax all over them? To avoid these hassles, set clear boundaries and explain to friends that you don't lend them out.

Day 47

It's never too early to start thinking about housing for next year.

Start exploring your housing options for the following year as soon as possible—on-campus dorms, off-campus apartments, or shared housing. By starting early, you can avoid the stress of last-minute searches and have more time to find the perfect place. Keep an eye on deadlines and application processes for on-campus housing and research the best off-campus options well before the semester ends. This proactive approach allows you to get the jump on others and discuss living arrangements with future roommates.

Day 48

Learning to ask for help is a sign of self-awareness.

Asking for help isn't a weakness—it's a power move. Whether it's turning to your parents, a trusted friend, or another adult you respect, learning to ask for support shows self-awareness and maturity. It means you recognize when you need guidance and take action to get it. This skill will serve you well in college, where challenges pop up—academically, socially, or emotionally. No one expects you to handle everything alone, and reaching out shows strength, not failure. Practice now, and you'll be ready to confidently tackle whatever college throws your way.

Day 49

If you're driving to school, know how to change a flat tire.

College life can be unpredictable, and having basic car maintenance skills can save you time and money. Knowing how to change a tire means you won't have to wait for roadside assistance if you get a flat, which can be especially handy in a remote area or on a tight schedule. You can find tutorials online or ask a family member to show you the ropes before you head off to school. Mastering these basics prepares you for unexpected situations and helps you feel more independent. Plus, do you need someone's help to refill your wiper fluid?

Day 50

Learn to make your own doctor and dentist appointments.

Being able to schedule these appointments yourself is a big step towards independence. Start by familiarizing yourself with how to contact healthcare providers and what information you must provide. Learn to check your insurance coverage and understand what's included in your plan. Making appointments can also teach you to manage your time effectively and balance your academic schedule with your health needs. Don't be afraid to make a few calls or send emails to get comfortable with the process.

Day 51

Work hard and save as much as possible over the summer, then budget during the school year.

College can be expensive, and having a financial cushion will make a big difference. Use school breaks to get a summer job, take on extra shifts, or even do some freelance work to build up your savings. Once the school year begins, put your budgeting skills to work. Track your expenses, plan how much you can spend each month, and stick to it. Use budgeting apps or a simple spreadsheet to monitor your income and expenses. Allocate funds for essentials like food and textbooks, and you won't have to keep asking mom or dad for a few bucks.

Day 52

Train yourself in various memory techniques before college begins.

College will throw a lot of information your way, so it's important to find study and memory techniques that work best for you. Everyone's brain processes information differently, so experimenting with different methods can help you discover what boosts your retention and focus. Some techniques are great for memorizing facts, while others help with understanding complex concepts. By learning and practicing these strategies before college starts, you'll walk in with tools to make your study sessions more effective and less stressful. This not only helps when exams and deadlines pile up but also improves your ability to manage time, stay organized, and keep track of assignments. Developing strong memory skills now sets the foundation for academic success later.

If you're looking to level up your study sessions, here are a few advanced memory techniques to add to your tool kit.

The Method of Loci (Memory Palace): This technique involves visualizing a familiar place, like your dorm room or childhood home, and mentally placing the information you want to remember in specific locations within that space. When you need to recall the information, you "walk" through the memory palace in your mind, retrieving the details from where you placed them. This method works well for memorizing lists, speeches, or key points for exams.

The Feynman Technique: Named after physicist Richard Feynman, this technique helps deepen understanding and memory by teaching a concept in simple terms, as if explaining it to someone with no background in the subject. Break the topic down, avoid jargon, and identify gaps in your understanding. This active process strengthens neural connections, making it easier to recall complex information during exams.

Spaced Repetition: This technique uses increasing intervals of time between study sessions to reinforce memory. Tools like Anki or Quizlet use algorithms to help you review material just before you're likely to forget it, maximizing long-term retention. Spaced repetition is especially effective for vocabulary, formulas, and key facts that need to stick for the long haul.

Acronyms and Acrostics: Using acronyms (like PEMDAS for the order of operations: Parentheses, Exponents, Multiplication, Division, Addition, Subtraction) or acrostics (creating sentences where the first letter of each word helps you remember a sequence) can simplify complex information. This technique is especially helpful for memorizing lists, steps in a process, or sequences in science and math.

Visualization: Creating mental images to represent information can make it more memorable. The more vivid and detailed the image, the better. For example, if you're trying to remember the parts of a cell, imagine each part as a character in a story—the nucleus as a boss giving orders, the mitochondria as power generators, and so on. Connecting facts to creative visuals helps lock them into your memory.

Day 53

Create a move-in day plan with your parents to avoid stress.

Move-in day can feel overwhelming, but creating a plan with your parents ahead of time can make it smoother and less stressful. Start by assigning specific tasks. Ask one person to take photos of the room before unpacking to document any damage for the housing office. Another can help with cleaning the space. If you've ordered items from local stores or forgotten anything, assign someone as the "runner" to grab those while the rest of you unpack. If furniture needs assembling, let one person focus on that while you organize your belongings. Bring a checklist to ensure you don't forget essentials and have a small toolkit handy for any last-minute needs. Taking charge of the plan shows your parents you're ready for independence while keeping things efficient and calm.

Day 54

Prepare in advance how you will handle the pressure of drugs and alcohol.

Navigating the social scene in college often involves encountering situations where you will likely feel pressured to experiment with drugs or alcohol. Thinking about how you'll respond before you find yourself in those situations is important. Decide on your boundaries and rehearse your responses to potential pressure. A plan can help you stay true to your values and avoid making choices you might regret. Surround yourself with friends who support your decisions.

Chapter 2

Find Your Footing: Adjusting to College Life

Day 55

During the first two weeks of school, say yes to every invitation and event.

This is your chance to meet new people, explore different activities, and find your place on campus. Whether it's a club meeting, a dorm hangout, a random campus event, or just a walk to grab coffee with someone, say yes! You'll never know where these experiences might lead. College is all about creating connections, and the first couple of weeks are a great time for that. You'll have plenty of time later to settle into a routine, but in the beginning, be open to everything. Even if something feels a bit out of your comfort zone, give it a shot, you might discover a new hobby or make a close friend.

Tip: Even if you don't connect in the first few weeks, there are plenty of opportunities throughout your entire first year to meet and make new friends.

Day 56

Be yourself; everyone else is already taken.

In college, you'll meet people from all walks of life, and it can be tempting to try and fit in by changing who you are. But here's the thing: the best way to attract the right friends, opportunities, and experiences is by being true to yourself. Pretending to be someone you're not will only lead to stress and confusion, and people can usually tell when someone's being fake. Embrace your quirks, interests, and values, even if they don't match the crowd. It's okay if you're into things that others might find unusual—that's what makes you unique. College is about discovering more about yourself, not losing yourself in the process.

Day 57

Problems on the back burner are sure to boil over.

Addressing issues early—whether they're related to academics, relationships, or personal struggles—can prevent them from piling up and becoming overwhelming. It might feel uncomfortable to face challenges head-on, but doing so often reveals they're not as daunting as they first seemed. Talk to someone you trust, like a friend, parent, professor, or counselor, or break tasks into smaller steps to make them more manageable. Whether it's clarifying a confusing topic with an instructor, resolving a conflict with a roommate, or seeking support for personal challenges, taking action sooner rather than later keeps small problems from growing into major crises.

Day 58

If living in the dorm, don't expect much quiet or privacy.

Dorms are busy places with a lot of people coming and going, so don't expect it to be a peaceful retreat. Noise from hallways, common areas, and other rooms is part of the package. Privacy can be limited too, as you'll likely share a room and common spaces with one or more roommates. Make sure to establish boundaries and communicate openly with your roommates to manage your shared space. As for cleanliness, dorms can be hit or miss, so take responsibility for your own area and pitch in with communal chores to keep things as tidy as possible. Embrace the lively atmosphere of dorm life because it might not be perfect, but it's all part of the adventure.

Day 59

You don't have to ask permission to go to the bathroom.

No professor expects you to raise your hand or explain why you need to leave the room. If nature calls and you need a quick bio-break, quietly get up and head out—just be respectful. Don't make it a habit of leaving during important parts of the lecture, and try not to be disruptive when you walk out or come back in. Professors are generally cool with this because they know you're a responsible adult. If you miss something, it's on you to catch up. Just remember to be courteous, and if it's a smaller class or a more interactive one, try to leave during a natural break in the discussion.

Day 60

Do not transfer after the first semester.

The first few months of college can be tough as you adjust to a new environment, new people, and a new way of learning. It's common to feel overwhelmed or homesick, but these feelings often ease as you get used to your routine and build connections. Give yourself time to settle in and find your groove. Transferring might seem like an easy solution, but it can be just as challenging to start over somewhere else. Instead, focus on making the most of the situation you're in. Get involved in campus activities, seek out support from advisors or counselors, and give yourself the chance to adapt. College is a big transition, and it's normal to have a rough start. With time, you'll likely find that things improve.

Day 61

You don't need to be best friends with your roommate.

College is about meeting new people, and sometimes that means sharing a space with someone you don't click with on a personal level. Focus on respect and communication. Set clear boundaries and keep your space organized to make living together more manageable. You can still have a positive relationship by being polite, listening, and supporting each other when needed. If you do end up forming a close friendship with your roommate, that's great, but it's not a requirement. College is a time to discover yourself and connect with many different people, so don't stress if you and your roommate don't become best buds.

Day 62

Check your email often!

Your inbox will become a crucial hub for important information, from class updates and assignment deadlines to campus events and emergency alerts. Professors, advisors, and campus offices will communicate with you through email, so staying on top of it ensures you won't miss any critical details or opportunities. Set aside specific times each day to read and respond to your emails, and make sure to check it at least once in the morning and once in the evening. If you receive a message requiring action, address it promptly to avoid falling behind. Utilize email management tools to keep your inbox organized. You can also create folders or labels for different types of messages to easily find what you need. It's smart to keep your school email separate from your personal email.

Day 63

Agree on cleaning responsibilities with your roommates.

When you move in, sit down together and discuss how to divide up chores fairly. Create a cleaning schedule that outlines who is responsible for what tasks and when they should be done. You don't have to write it down, but it's important you both agree. This might include taking out the trash, sweeping the floors, or cleaning the bathroom and microwave. Having a clear plan helps prevent misunderstandings and ensures that everyone contributes equally. Clear communication is key—talk openly about your expectations and listen to your roommates' preferences.

Day 64

Don't spend all your free time in your dorm.

It's tempting to stay holed up in your room, especially when you're tired or overwhelmed, but stepping out is key to making the most of college life. Explore campus, attend events, and engage in activities that interest you. Join clubs, participate in sports, or volunteer for causes you care about. This helps you build connections, discover new passions, and find your place in the college community. The more you get involved, the richer your experience will be. Socializing and experiencing new things outside of your dorm can also help you manage stress and prevent feelings of isolation.

Day 65

Address issues with your roommate early on.

When something bothers you, speak up about it sooner rather than later. If you wait too long, small annoyances can build up and lead to unnecessary conflicts. Start with a calm and honest conversation, choose a good time when you're both relaxed and not in the heat of the moment. Use "I" statements to express your feelings without sounding accusatory. For example, say "I feel frustrated when the dishes are left in the sink" instead of "You never do the dishes." Listen to your roommate's side and be open to finding a compromise. Addressing problems right away helps you maintain a positive relationship and ensures that you both understand each other's boundaries and preferences.

Day 66

It's normal to have disagreements with your roommate.

When you share a space with someone new, differences in habits, schedules, and personal quirks can lead to disagreements. Don't stress out if conflicts arise; they're a common experience and can help you learn how to communicate better. The key is to handle these disputes constructively. Address issues directly, but respectfully, and try to see things from your roommate's perspective. Remember, it's not about winning an argument but about finding common ground and creating a comfortable living environment for both of you. Keep the lines of communication open and focus on solutions rather than dwelling on the problem.

Day 67

Keep your computer files organized, too!

Keeping your computer files organized is as important as managing your physical belongings. Create a clear folder structure for your classes, assignments, and personal projects. Label your folders with descriptive names and use subfolders to keep related documents together. Make a habit of organizing new files as soon as you create or download them, so you don't end up with a cluttered desktop or a chaotic downloads folder. Delete or archive files you no longer need to free up space and reduce digital clutter. Keeping your files in order will save you time when searching for essential documents and help you stay focused on your work without distractions.

Day 68

Tap into the career center early and often.

From your first semester, you can use the career center to explore different majors, discover what careers align with your interests, and even get help building a stand-out resume. They offer workshops on interviewing skills, networking events, and job fairs where you can meet potential employers. The career center is also a great place to find internships, which are key to gaining real-world experience and making connections in your field. Don't just think of it as a place to visit when looking for a job, it's a resource that can guide you throughout your college experience. The earlier you start using the career center, the more prepared you'll be when it's time to step into the job market.

Day 69

If it sounds too good to be true might be a scam.

Scammers often prey on students with offers of easy money, fake job opportunities, or unbelievable deals. They use flashy ads or urgent messages to create a sense of excitement or fear, pushing you to act quickly without thinking. Always take a step back and assess whether an offer seems realistic. If unsure, do a quick online search to see if others have reported similar scams or consult a trusted friend or advisor. It's perfectly okay to be skeptical and to ask questions. Never give out personal information, like your Social Security number or bank details, unless you're sure the request is legitimate.

Day 70

Over-prepare, then go with the flow.

When heading off to college, planning and preparing for everything you can is smart—buying supplies, organizing your schedule, and researching your classes. This preparation will give you a solid foundation and make you feel more confident. However, understand that not everything will go according to plan. College life is full of surprises, and you'll face unexpected challenges and opportunities. Once you've done your homework and packed your bags, let go of the need for everything to be perfect. Embrace flexibility and adapt to new situations as they arise. If you encounter a change in your schedule or a hiccup with your dorm room, stay calm and adjust as needed.

Day 71

Wash your sheets and towels often.

Aim to wash your sheets at least once every two weeks. Dirty sheets can attract dust mites and allergens, making it harder for you to sleep well. Towels should be washed after a few uses to prevent bacteria buildup and unpleasant odors. Keeping up with this routine helps maintain good hygiene and keeps your dorm room smelling fresh. Make it a habit to set a specific day each week for laundry so it doesn't pile up and become overwhelming. If you share laundry facilities, consider investing in a laundry bag to keep your items organized and avoid mix-ups.

Day 72

Make sure the habits you pick up are positive and healthy.

When you start college, you'll naturally develop routines and behaviors. Use this opportunity to form habits that benefit your well-being and success. For example, establish a routine for studying that includes regular breaks and a quiet workspace. Incorporate physical activity into your schedule to keep your energy up and stress levels down. Choose to spend time with people who uplift and motivate you, rather than those who bring negativity. Good habits like maintaining a balanced diet, getting enough sleep, and managing your time effectively will set you up for success and keep you feeling your best. Pay attention to how you handle stress and make it a point to practice mindfulness or relaxation techniques if needed.

Day 73

Don't stop taking medications once you get to school.

Stopping medication suddenly or neglecting to take it as directed can have serious consequences for your health. Set reminders or use apps to help you stay on track with your medication. If you need assistance or have concerns about your medications, don't hesitate to contact the campus health center or a healthcare professional. Taking care of your health is essential to managing the demands of college life effectively and ensuring you're at your best, both academically and personally.

Day 74

Talk to your advisor a minimum of once or twice a year.

Your advisor isn't just there for emergencies or when you're in a bind—they're a valuable resource. Regular check-ins can keep you on track with your major requirements, help you explore minors or double majors, and even ensure you meet all the prerequisites for graduation. Take time to build a relationship with your advisor as it will strengthen the support you receive. Your advisor can also offer advice on course selection, helping you balance your workload and choose classes that align with your career goals. If you're unsure about your major, they can provide insight and resources to help you explore other options. To make your meetings effective, come prepared with your questions and your thoughts, then be ready for a great discussion.

Day 75

Tuition bills are sent to the student; do NOT ignore them!

When you receive your tuition statement, paying attention and addressing it promptly is crucial. Ignoring these bills can lead to late fees, holds on your account, and even interruptions to your classes or access to campus resources. Make a habit of checking your student account regularly for any updates or changes to your bill. If you encounter any issues or confusion with the billing, contact the financial aid office or bursar's office for assistance.

Day 76

Take advantage of security escorts.

Don't let pride or the fear of looking "uncool" stop you from taking advantage of security escorts on campus. It's not lame to prioritize your safety; it's brilliant. Whether you're walking back to your dorm late at night after a study session, heading to your car in a poorly lit parking lot, or just feeling uneasy, calling for a security escort is a resource designed to keep you safe. College campuses can be enormous, and while most are generally safe, there's no harm in being extra cautious. It's easy to forget that your safety should always come first, especially when trying to fit in and seem independent.

Day 77

Lock your valuables!

Safety and security are crucial, whether you're at home or away. Taking these simple precautions can protect you from theft and ensure your belongings are safe. Locking your door is the first line of defense against unauthorized entry. Make it a habit to check that all doors and windows are securely locked, especially before leaving your dorm or apartment. For your valuables, invest in a secure safe to store important items like jewelry, documents, and cash. A safe not only protects against theft but also adds a layer of security against potential accidents or natural disasters. While you may trust your roommate, you have no control over who else might be visiting your room.

Day 78

If you're overwhelmed, ask others how they keep organized.

Staying organized is key to surviving college, and if you're feeling overwhelmed, don't be afraid to ask others how they manage. You're not the only one who might struggle to juggle classes, assignments, extracurriculars, and maybe even a job. Find a system that works for you, whether it's using a planner, digital calendar, or even sticky notes plastered all over your desk. The important thing is to have a plan and stick to it. But if you find yourself drowning in deadlines and to-do lists, reach out to a classmate, your RA, or even your professor, they might have tips that could save you from a late-night panic. Everyone has their own method, and you might discover something that makes your life a whole lot easier.

Day 79

Don't take on commitments just because you think it will look good on a resume.

Choose commitments that align with your passions and career goals. It's better to engage deeply in a few activities where you can gain meaningful experiences, than to spread yourself too thin. Taking on too many obligations can lead to burnout, lower your performance in each area, and diminish the overall quality of your work. Instead, focus on areas where you can develop skills, build relationships, and contribute effectively.

Day 80

Scope out the campus medical facility before you need it.

It might not be the first thing on your mind when you arrive at college but knowing where to go when you're not feeling your best can save you a lot of stress later. Find out where the health center is located and what services they offer. Do they have walk-in hours, or do you need an appointment? Are there certain days when the facility is closed? Make sure you know how to contact them in case of an emergency. Some campuses also offer mental health services, so check if that's available too. It's better to have all this information before you're in a situation where you need it.

Day 81

Save campus security and police phone numbers.

Emergencies don't send you a warning, and in those moments, you don't want to waste precious time searching for the right contact information. By having emergency numbers saved and easily accessible, you're giving yourself a safety net that could make all the difference. Don't just assume you'll never need them, preparation is key. Even if you never use them, knowing they're there will give you peace of mind. Plus, it's one less thing to worry about when you're already juggling new classes, friends, and all the other pressures of college life. Safety isn't just about avoiding trouble; it's about being ready to act when something unexpected happens. So, take two minutes, add those numbers to your contacts, and then forget about them—until you need them.

Day 82

Pick up a part time job; just not during your first semester.

Picking up a part-time job on campus is a great way to earn some extra cash and get involved in the college community, but it's best to wait until your second semester starts. The first semester is all about adjusting to college life, settling into your classes, and figuring out your new routine. Adding a job to the mix too soon can overwhelm you and affect your academic performance. Instead, focus on finding your balance and learning how to manage your time effectively. Once you've got a handle on your coursework and campus life, investigate part-time job opportunities that fit your schedule and interests. Many colleges offer flexible positions that accommodate student schedules, from working in the library to assisting in campus events.

Day 83

Organize your email!

Your inbox will fill quickly with messages from professors, advisors, clubs, and even the financial aid office. If you don't stay organized, it's easy to miss critical information. Start by creating folders or labels for different categories, like classes, bills, and campus events. This way, you can quickly sort your emails and find what you need when you need it. Set up filters to automatically route certain emails to specific folders, keeping your main inbox clutter-free. Make it a habit to check your email daily and flag what might require a follow-up, so you won't forget.

Day 84

Keep your computer anti-virus up to date.

Cybersecurity is constantly changing, with new viruses, malware, and other malicious software emerging all the time. An updated anti-virus program helps safeguard your system by detecting and neutralizing these threats before they can cause harm. Make it a habit to check for and install updates frequently, as these updates include the latest security patches and improvements. Keeping your anti-virus software current not only protects your data and personal information, but also ensures your computer runs smoothly and efficiently. Don't wait until you encounter a problem—be proactive about your digital security to prevent issues before they arise.

Day 85

It's going to take time to become familiar with your school.

Starting at a new school can feel overwhelming with all the new faces, places, and routines. Give yourself permission to settle in gradually and don't stress about having everything figured out right away. Explore your new environment at your own pace, and soon, things will start to feel more comfortable and familiar. Engage with campus resources, attend orientation events, and connect with fellow students to help speed up the process. The more you immerse yourself, the quicker you'll find your rhythm. Be patient with yourself and enjoy the journey of discovering your new school.

Day 86

Introduce yourself to the professors.

Making the effort to connect with your professors early on can have a big impact on your academic experience. Start by introducing yourself and expressing your interest in their course. This helps build a positive relationship and shows that you're proactive about your education. Additionally, ask for their office hours and make a note of them. Office hours are a valuable opportunity for one-on-one interaction, where you can ask questions, seek clarification on course material, or discuss academic concerns. Building these connections can also be beneficial for networking and future recommendations.

Day 87

Vinegar in the wash cycle will freshen musty towels.

If your towels start smelling musty, don't panic, there's a simple fix. Just add some vinegar to your wash cycle. Musty odors often happen because towels don't fully dry out, allowing mildew to develop. To tackle this issue, pour a cup of white vinegar into the washing machine's fabric softener dispenser or directly into the drum. Vinegar works as a natural deodorizer and helps to break down any mold or mildew causing the smell. Run your towels through a regular wash cycle with your usual detergent, and make sure to dry them thoroughly afterward.

Day 88

If you can live harmoniously with someone in a 20' x 20' space, you can do anything.

Sharing such a small space requires a lot of patience, flexibility, and open communication. You'll learn quickly how to navigate differences, whether it's deciding who gets the top bunk or how to share limited closet space. You'll also figure out how to manage different schedules, study habits, and personal quirks without driving each other crazy. The experience will teach you valuable skills like compromise, empathy, and conflict resolution—skills that will serve you well in any relationship, whether it's with future roommates, coworkers, or partners.

Day 89

Focus on a few new things rather than juggling a ton.

When you start college, it's tempting to dive into everything at once: clubs, sports, social events, and academic challenges. Focusing on a few new things, instead of juggling a ton, will help you make the most of your time and energy. Choose a couple of activities or interests that genuinely excite you and put your heart into them. Whether it's joining a campus club, exploring a new hobby, or taking on a leadership role, concentrating on fewer commitments allows you to develop deeper connections and skills. You'll find that you perform better and feel more fulfilled when you're not stretched too thin. Plus, managing a smaller number of activities helps you maintain balance to avoid burnout.

Day 90

Find cheap or free forms of transportation.

Instead of relying on a car or expensive rideshares, consider options like biking, using campus shuttles, or taking advantage of public transit. Many colleges offer free or low-cost shuttle services that cover popular routes, making it easy to get around without spending a fortune. Biking is another great cost-effective choice that helps you stay fit and reduce your carbon footprint. Look into bike-sharing programs on campus or nearby, which can be a convenient and affordable way to get around. Public transportation is also worth exploring; many cities offer discounted student passes that make commuting more budget friendly.

Day 91

Don't turn to shopping as a stress reliever.

When college life gets overwhelming, it's tempting to turn to shopping as a quick stress reliever, but this habit can lead to financial strain and doesn't address the root of the problem. Instead of hitting the mall or online stores for comfort, try healthier, more sustainable ways to manage stress. Learning effective stress management techniques, such as mindfulness and time management, can help you stay on top of your responsibilities without resorting to impulse buying. By addressing stress through positive actions, you'll maintain better control over your finances and develop healthier coping strategies that will serve you well beyond college.

Day 92

Don't lend something you are not willing to lose.

When you lend an item, there's always a risk it might not come back, or it might come back damaged. If you're really attached to something like your favorite hoodie, expensive headphones, or a sentimental book, consider keeping it to yourself. Before you lend something, ask yourself if you can handle the possibility of it not being returned in the same condition, or at all. It's not about distrusting others; it's about setting boundaries to protect your possessions and your peace of mind. If you're okay with the chance of losing or damaging the item, then go ahead and lend it. But if it's something you really care about, just don't lend it out.

Day 93

Avoid early morning classes.

Early morning classes might seem like a good idea when you're planning your schedule, but waking up for a 7AM class after a late night of studying (or hanging out) isn't as easy as it sounds. College offers more freedom, and with that comes the temptation to stay up later. While early classes can seem productive, they often leave you groggy and unfocused, making it tough to retain what you're learning. Instead, aim for mid-morning or early afternoon classes so you're more rested and alert. A little extra sleep can go a long way in helping you balance academics, social life, and just enjoying the college experience!

Day 94

Call or text your parents at least once a week.

Call or text your parents at least once a week, it's not just for them, but for you too. Staying in touch regularly helps keep your relationship strong and gives them peace of mind, which in turn might help them loosen their grip a bit. If they know you're doing okay, they're less likely to hover or worry excessively. It's a simple gesture that goes a long way. Just a quick message or call to let them know you're handling things can make all the difference. They'll appreciate the effort, and you'll likely find that they start to trust you more as they see you're managing college life well. It's a small act, but it shows that you care, even from a distance. And who knows? You might find that those conversations give you a little extra support and encouragement when you need it most.

Day 95

Get off your phone and engage with the world around you.

It's tempting to stay glued to your phone, but I beg you... put it down and engage with your surroundings! College is full of opportunities that you'll miss if you're always staring at a screen. You don't want to overlook meeting new people, exploring campus, or jumping into fun activities because you're distracted by social media. Getting involved means more than just attending class—it's about showing up, making connections, and discovering what your school has to offer. Your phone will still be there, but those real-life experiences won't, so take advantage of them and dive in!

Day 96

Don't expect college to be a four-year vacation.

Don't fall into the trap of thinking college is a four-year vacation, it's a lot of hard work. While freedom and new experiences are exciting, they come with responsibilities. College demands focus, dedication, and perseverance. From managing challenging coursework to juggling extracurricular activities, you'll need to stay on top of your game. Balancing study time with social activities requires discipline, and procrastination can quickly lead to stress. Set clear goals, develop strong study habits, and keep up with assignments to avoid last-minute cramming. Remember, college is not just about fun; it's about preparing for your future.

Day 97

Do laundry during off hours.

Do laundry during off hours to save yourself a lot of hassle and time. If you wait until the weekend or peak times, you'll be stuck waiting for machines, dealing with crowded laundry rooms, and possibly even finding your wet clothes dumped out by someone impatient. Instead, figure out when the laundry room is usually empty—early mornings, late at night, or during big campus events when everyone else is out—and make that your regular laundry time. You'll have your pick of machines, won't have to rush, and can avoid any laundry-related stress. Plus, if you do it during off hours, you might get some peace and quiet, a rarity in college life.

Day 98

Always ask if you want to borrow something and communicate when something is bothering you.

Always ask before borrowing anything, whether it's a textbook, phone charger, or even a snack. This simple act of respect keeps things running smoothly between you and your roommate or friends. It shows that you value their belongings and appreciate their trust. On the flip side, if something is bothering you, like someone taking your stuff without asking or any other issue, speak up. Communication is key to avoiding resentment and keeping your living situation comfortable. It might feel awkward at first, but addressing problems early prevents them from becoming more significant issues later. Be transparent and honest about what's on your mind.

Day 99

Avoid time wasters like TV, video games and social media.

While these can be fun and relaxing, they often waste valuable time spent on more productive activities. Instead of letting these distractions take over your day, create a balanced schedule that includes time for studying, socializing, exercising, and pursuing hobbies. Setting specific limits for your time for social media, even fifteen minutes a day, can help you stay focused and maintain a healthy balance. Use your time wisely to build skills, connect with people, and explore new interests.

Day 100

If you find yourself feeling lost, lonely or bored, get out of your dorm and explore the campus.

If you find yourself feeling lost, lonely, or bored, don't just sit in your dorm waiting for things to change. Instead, get out and explore your campus. There's always something happening, whether it's a club meeting, a sports event, or just students hanging out at the student center. College campuses are full of energy and opportunities, but you have to step out of your comfort zone to find them. Walk around, check out the bulletin boards, or follow your school's social media pages to see what's going on. Even if you just take a walk around the campus, you'll feel more connected to your surroundings and remind yourself that you are part of a bigger community.

Day 101

Ask for the student discount everywhere you go.

Simply asking if a discount is available can save you money on everything from textbooks and clothes to meals and movie tickets. Keep your student ID handy and don't be afraid to mention it when making a purchase. Some businesses might not advertise their student discounts, so it's worth asking every time you shop. You might be surprised at how much you can save just by taking a moment to inquire. By making it a habit to ask for discounts, you can stretch your budget further and enjoy your college experience without breaking the bank.

Chapter 3

Degrees Don't Earn Themselves:
Staying Focused on What Matters Most

Day 102

Yes, there are ways to get into a full class.

Professors appreciate students who are motivated, engaged, and ready to contribute. If a class you really need or want is at capacity, don't be discouraged, reach out to the professor. Politely explain why you're interested in the course and how you're prepared to be an active, dedicated student. Mention any specific reasons the class is important for your academic goals. Be respectful and clear that you understand the situation, but also show your enthusiasm. Professors often have the final say on who gets into their class, and if they see that you're serious, responsible, and willing to go the extra mile, they might just make room for you. Sometimes persistence and a positive attitude can get you opportunities that seem closed off at first. Just remember to approach it with humility and professionalism, you're asking for a favor, but your effort and enthusiasm could be what tips the scales in your favor.

Tip: When you do get into that class, don't slack off because you'll be burning a bridge with the professor.

Day 103

STDs are nobody's friend.

Protecting yourself and your partner from sexually transmitted infections (STIs) is crucial. Condoms significantly reduce the risk of STIs and unintended pregnancies, offering a layer of safety that shouldn't be overlooked. STIs can have serious health consequences and can be spread easily, so taking this simple step can safeguard your well-being. It's not just about preventing diseases; it's about showing respect for yourself and your partner. Always keep condoms handy and use them consistently, regardless of the situation or your partner's assurances. Being prepared is part of being responsible.

Day 104

Know that time is your most valuable asset.

As you head to college, you'll face countless opportunities and challenges, and how you manage your time will determine your success. Prioritize tasks, set clear goals, and avoid procrastination. Balance your academic responsibilities with social activities and personal downtime. Avoid consuming your time with distractions like excessive social media use or last-minute cramming, Instead, focus on activities that contribute to your growth, such as studying, exercising, and engaging in meaningful relationships. Keep a planner or use digital tools to track deadlines, appointments, and goals. By being intentional with your time, you'll find yourself more productive and less stressed.

Day 105

Get up on time so you don't start the day rushed.

Set your alarm for a time that gives you plenty of space to get ready at a comfortable pace, so you can have a relaxed breakfast, review your schedule, and mentally prepare for the day ahead. Rushing out the door can lead to forgotten items and unnecessary stress. By establishing a consistent morning routine, you create a sense of stability and control over your day. Organize your things the night before, such as packing your backpack and laying out your clothes, to make your morning even smoother. Embrace the calm that comes with being on time, or early, and you'll set a positive tone for your day.

Day 106

Stick to one solid system to stay organized.

When trying to stay organized, choose a method that works best for you, whether it's a digital calendar, a physical planner, or a combination of both. Consistency is key. Use this system for tracking assignments, deadlines, and appointments. By relying on a single approach, you'll avoid confusion and ensure that nothing slips through the cracks. If you opt for a digital solution, use apps and tools that sync across your devices to keep everything up to date. If you prefer a physical planner, always keep it with you and make it a habit to jot down important dates and tasks. Regularly review and update your system to adapt to your schedule changes.

Day 107

Expect to be homesick at some level.

Being homesick is a normal part of the transition and you might miss your family, friends, and your hometown. To help manage these feelings, stay busy and dive into campus life. Join clubs, attend events, and explore your new surroundings. Connecting with people and finding friends who share your interests and experiences is key. Building a new support network will help you feel more at home and less isolated. Keep yourself engaged with activities and responsibilities, which will not only distract you from homesickness but also help you create a fulfilling college experience. Over time, homesickness will fade as you become more accustomed to your new environment and routine.

Day 108

Budget is not a four-letter word.

It's tempting to swipe your credit card for ordinary purchases like coffee or late-night snacks, but that can quickly lead to debt that's hard to shake off. Instead, set a realistic budget that covers your essentials while leaving room for some fun and unexpected expenses. Stick to using cash or a debit card for everyday purchases so you can keep track of how much you're spending and avoid overspending. Credit cards should be reserved for emergencies or planned big expenses that you can pay off right away. Being mindful of your spending now means you won't be drowning in debt later.

Day 109

Have fun, but stay true to yourself.

While it's important to enjoy yourself and make the most of your college years, don't let the fun take over your priorities. Stay true to yourself, your values, and the goals you set when you decided to go to college. Remember, your family has your back, and they believe in you. Keep their support in mind when things get tough or when you're tempted to stray from your path. Have fun, meet new people, and explore new interests, but always keep your eye on the bigger picture. Your degree is your ticket to the future you want, and it's worth the effort. Make decisions that align with your goals, and don't forget why you came to college in the first place.

Day 110

Get involved with things that interest you, not the crowd.

You don't have to know exactly what you want right away; just dive into things that spark your interest. Not only will you meet new people who share your passions, but you'll also develop skills and connections that will serve you well beyond college. These experiences can help you grow as a person, build your confidence, and even make your resume stand out. So, take the leap, try new activities, challenge yourself, and get involved. The more you engage with your campus community, the more you'll feel at home and the more memories you'll create. Plus, who knows? You might discover a new passion or even a potential career path.

Day 111

Be part of something bigger than yourself.

Whether volunteering for a cause you care about, joining a student organization, or getting involved in community service, finding ways to contribute to something that matters. When you're part of a group working toward a common goal, you'll experience a sense of purpose beyond just getting a degree. You'll learn to collaborate, understand different perspectives, and make an impact that can last long after graduation. Plus, being involved in something larger than yourself helps you build a network of like-minded people who can become lifelong friends or professional contacts. Not only will you grow personally, but you'll also help create a better community around you.

Day 112

NO means Next Opportunity.

College will throw plenty of closed doors your way, whether it's a rejection from a club, a missed internship, or a failed attempt at something new. The important thing is how you respond. Don't dwell on what didn't happen; focus on what could happen next. Every "NO" is a step closer to the right "YES." Use rejection as motivation to find new paths, explore different options, and grow stronger. If one opportunity doesn't work out, it just means something else, maybe even better, is waiting for you. Keep pushing forward with your head held high.

Day 113

Foot fungus is funky... and hard to get rid of!

Always wear flip-flops in communal showers—trust me, foot fungus is the last thing you want to bring back to your dorm. Those showers are a breeding ground for all kinds of germs, and it's way too easy to pick up something nasty if you're not careful. Foot fungus is not only uncomfortable but also stubborn and can be tricky to get rid of. Plus, it's just plain gross. Protect your feet by making flip-flops a non-negotiable part of your shower routine. It might seem like a small thing, but it's a smart move that'll save you a lot of trouble down the line. So, don't take any chances—slip them on before you step in and keep your feet happy and healthy.

Day 114

Be prepared to feel lost. It's natural. Just be sure to reach out to friends who can pull you out of your funk.

Feeling lost is a normal part of starting college. It's normal to feel a bit overwhelmed or unsure at times. What's important is that you don't keep those feelings to yourself. Reach out to old and new friends who can help you navigate these rough patches. Sometimes, a quick chat or hanging out can lift your spirits and give you a fresh perspective. Don't hesitate to lean on your support network when things get tough; they've likely been through similar struggles and can offer valuable advice and comfort. Remember, it's part of the college experience to encounter bumps along the road, and seeking support is a sign of strength, not weakness.

Day 115

Get contact information for your roommate's family.

Getting your roommate's family contact information is a smart move. It's like having an extra safety net in case something comes up. By sharing contact details, you create an open line of communication that can be useful in emergencies or if you need to reach out for any reason. For instance, if there's a problem with your roommate that you can't resolve on your own, having a direct way to contact their family can help. Plus, it's a nice way to build a bridge with your roommate's support system, making it easier to address any issues.

Day 116

People size you up quickly, so make sure the impression you leave is positive and one you're proud of.

Your school might feel enormous at first, but trust me, it's not as big as you think. People will start to recognize you and form opinions about you quickly. That's why it's crucial to be mindful of the image you project. From the get-go, aim to present yourself positively and authentically. Whether through your actions, your attitude, or the way you interact with others, make sure you're proud of the impression you're leaving. Remember, how you behave now can shape how people see you throughout your college experience. If you're not careful and let negative behaviors slip through, they can stick with you for all four years.

Day 117

This is the part where you find out who you are.

As you navigate new experiences and face challenges, you'll start discovering what truly matters to you. Embrace this opportunity to try new things, meet diverse people, and step outside your comfort zone. It's okay to feel uncertain or change your mind along the way; this exploration is crucial to personal growth. Allow yourself the freedom to make mistakes and learn from them. Surround yourself with supportive people who encourage your self-discovery. By the end of your college journey, you'll have a clearer sense of who you are and what you want out of life.

Day 118

Some days, everything is going your way; other days,
you feel like your world is crumbling.

Some days will feel like everything is falling into place: your classes go smoothly, you ace your exams, and life seems perfect. Other days, you might feel overwhelmed, like everything is going wrong and the world is crumbling around you. It's crucial to push through and keep moving forward on those tough days. Remember that challenges are a normal part of the college experience and part of growing. When you face setbacks, don't let them define your whole journey. Break your problems into smaller, manageable steps and tackle them one at a time. Use these tough moments to build resilience and learn more about yourself. Remember your long-term goals and remind yourself that tough times don't last forever.

Day 119

Don't suffer in silence.

Everyone has tough days, and talking about your feelings can be incredibly relieving. Find a trusted friend, family member, or counselor ready to listen and offer support. It's easy to keep your struggles to yourself but sharing what you're going through can lighten your emotional load and provide fresh perspectives. Don't hesitate to seek out resources available on campus, like counseling services or student support groups. Opening up might feel uncomfortable at first, but it's a crucial step in managing your mental health. Don't let isolation hold you back; act and talk to someone.

Day 120

Worrying is betting against yourself.

When you worry, you focus on what might go wrong instead of believing in your ability to handle challenges. It's easy to fall into the trap of imagining worst-case scenarios, but doing so only drains your energy and clouds your judgment. Instead of stressing over potential problems, channel your energy into preparing and problem-solving. Remind yourself that you've faced challenges before and come out stronger. Focusing on positive actions and solutions will boost your confidence and increase your chances of success. Worrying won't change outcomes; it only steals your peace of mind. Replace worry with proactive steps—plan, prepare, and act where possible.

Day 121

Create a solid morning routine.

Start by planning a wake-up time that gives you enough space to ease into your day without rushing. Incorporate activities that help you feel energized and focused—a quick workout, a nutritious breakfast, or a few minutes of meditation. Organize your tasks for the day, prioritize your most important ones, and get a head start on them before your schedule gets busy. Having a set routine helps you build momentum, reduces stress, and makes your mornings smoother. Sticking with it is crucial even when you don't feel like it; consistency is key.

Day 122

Slow down! Take your time.

Slow down and take things one step at a time as you dive into college life. It's easy to get caught up in the excitement and try to do everything at once, like joining every club, meeting everyone, and cramming your schedule. But jumping in too fast can quickly lead to burnout. Instead, focus on easing into your new environment. Pick a few activities or commitments that genuinely interest you and give yourself the space to adapt to your new routine. Balance is key. By pacing yourself, you'll have the chance to build meaningful connections, find your rhythm, and truly absorb all that college has to offer. Remember, it's not about how much you do but how well you do it. So, take a breath, set realistic goals, and allow yourself the time to adjust.

Day 123

Don't hook up too much in the first few weeks!

Diving into the social scene and seeking immediate connections is tempting, but rushing into hook-ups can lead to regrets and added stress. Use this time to focus on getting to know yourself and your surroundings better. Build meaningful friendships and find your footing academically and socially before jumping into anything physical. Starting college is a whirlwind of new experiences, making it easy to get swept up in excitement. By taking things slow, you'll have a clearer sense of what you truly want and who you genuinely connect with. The goal is to create lasting, authentic relationships rather than fleeting encounters.

Day 124

It will take time to acclimate.

Starting college means diving into a completely new environment, and it will be a shock to your system. Give yourself time to adjust and not rush the process. Embrace the change and be patient with yourself as you navigate this transition. Explore your campus, attend events, and slowly build a routine that works for you. It's all part of finding your footing in this new chapter of your life. Remember, everyone experiences this shift differently, and feeling out of place at first is completely normal. Allow yourself the grace to adapt at your own pace, and soon enough, what seems unfamiliar will become your new normal.

Day 125

A sound machine can be a saving grace.

In a busy college environment, a sound machine can be a lifesaver for creating a peaceful, focused study space and ensuring a good night's sleep. Whether you're dealing with noisy roommates, bustling hallways, or the general buzz of campus life, a sound machine helps mask disruptive noises with soothing background sounds like white noise or gentle nature sounds. This can improve concentration during study sessions and help you unwind and relax when it's time to sleep.

Day 126

It's OK to switch majors.

It's completely normal to switch majors in college, but before you make the jump, do your homework. Don't let a tough class or a single bad grade push you into making a snap decision. Instead, take the time to explore why you're thinking about switching. Talk to academic advisors, professors, and even students in the major you're considering. Ask about the workload, job prospects, and whether the courses align with your interests and strengths. Research what the new major will require in terms of classes and time commitment. Some majors may set you back a semester or more. It's also important to consider how the switch might impact your future, whether it's grad school or your career path. Changing majors isn't just about finding something easier; it's about finding something that excites you and fits with your long-term goals.

Day 127

The best seats in a lecture hall are the aisle seats.

Sitting on the aisle gives you a bit more space to stretch out, and you won't feel boxed in by other people. If you need to leave for any reason, whether it's a bathroom break or you need to step out to take a call, you can quietly slip out without having to crawl over a whole row of students. Plus, when the lecture ends, you'll be one of the first to leave, avoiding the mad rush of everyone trying to squeeze out at once. You'll also have a clear view of the professor and can quickly catch their eye if you have a question.

Day 128

Get a planner and write everything down!

Get yourself a planner and write everything down! It might sound old-school, but trust me, this will save you so much stress. Between classes, assignments, exams, club meetings, social events, and just everyday life, things can pile up fast. By writing everything down in one place—whether it's a physical planner or a digital one—you'll stay organized and on top of your responsibilities. You won't have to rely on your memory to keep track of deadlines or appointments, and you'll be less likely to forget important things. Plus, it's satisfying to check things off as you get them done. It also helps you see the bigger picture of how your week or month is shaping up, so you can manage your time better and avoid last-minute panic. Pro tip: color-code it or use stickers to feed your creative side.

Day 129

Get required classes done during your freshman year.

It might be tempting to put off required classes in favor of the fun, interesting ones. But trust me, getting those core requirements out of the way during your first year is one of the best moves you can make. By knocking out those general classes early, free up time in your later years to dive into the stuff you're passionate about. Plus, it's a lot easier to tackle subjects you're less enthusiastic about when you've got that fresh burst of energy. Future you will be so grateful when you're not cramming in a random science or math course senior year when you'd rather be focusing on your major. So, buckle down now, and you'll thank yourself later!

Day 130

Don't feel obligated to help everyone study.

You are going to meet all sorts of people with different study habits, and some may ask for your help. Here's a little secret: you're not obligated to be everyone's personal tutor. It's great to lend a hand when you can, but your time is valuable, and college is as much about managing it as it is about learning. Helping here and there is fine, but don't feel guilty for saying no when you need to focus on your own work. Plus, helping too much can lead to people relying on you instead of learning to stand on their own. Set boundaries early, and remember, you're there to get your degree, not everyone else's! Be generous with your support when it makes sense but protect your own study time like it's the last slice of pizza.

Day 131

Review the entire test before you answer any questions.

When you review the entire test, you get a sense of what's ahead: how many questions there are, where the challenging parts might be, and how much time you'll need for each section. This also helps you spot questions you know you can answer quickly, boosting your confidence right out of the gate. Plus, if you notice a tricky question, your brain can start working on it in the background while you tackle the easier ones first.

Day 132

Don't freak out if you fail a midterm.

One bad test doesn't define your entire academic future, and there's usually plenty of time to turn things around. Start by reaching out to your professor. Professors appreciate students who take responsibility, so ask for feedback on where you went wrong and how you can improve. See if there are opportunities for extra credit, retakes, or ways to boost your grade through upcoming assignments or participation. Next, assess your study habits. Maybe you weren't studying effectively, or you didn't give yourself enough time to really absorb the material. Adjust your approach by using office hours, forming a study group, or visiting the tutoring center. Sometimes, even small tweaks to how you prepare can make a big difference. Failing a midterm is just a bump in the road, not the end of it.

Day 133

If you're late for class, enter quietly and respectfully.

No one likes the person who storms in like they're starring in their own action movie. Instead, take a breath, open the door softly, and find the closest seat without making a scene. Don't be the one who slams down their backpack or tries to make excuses mid-lecture. Your professor won't appreciate the interruption, and neither will your classmates. Just slip in, get settled, and catch up as best you can. Life is filled with moments where you'll need to navigate tricky situations with grace, and this is a great way to practice.

Day 134

Let your true self shine through everything you do.

You're going to meet a lot of new people, and it can be tempting to mold yourself to fit in. But here's the thing—there's only one you, and that's your superpower. Be yourself unapologetically. Your unique perspective, personality, and beliefs will make you stand out, and that's good. Let your true self come through in class, clubs, or hanging out with friends. People respect authenticity, and you'll build stronger connections when you're not trying to be someone you're not. Plus, college is about finding your path, not copying someone else's. So, speak your mind, stand by your values, and don't be afraid to be a little different. The world needs your originality, so let it shine—you never know who you'll inspire!

Day 135

If you want to drop out, you must have a solid, logical plan.

Let's be honest: college is not for everyone. However, if you're considering dropping out, ensure you have a solid, logical life plan. Having a clear vision of what you want to do instead and how you will achieve it is crucial. Research your alternative paths, whether starting a business, entering the workforce, or pursuing vocational training. Create a detailed plan outlining your goals, steps to reach them, and how you will support yourself financially. Talk to mentors, career advisors, or professionals in your field of interest to gather insights and advice. A well-thought-out plan will help you stay focused and motivated and prove to others that you're making a strategic choice rather than acting impulsively.

Here are a few other things to consider:

- Clarify why you want to drop out. Are you struggling with academics, finances, mental health, or even lack of interest.

- Explore alternatives to dropping out. See if you can take a leave of absence, or pursue college part-time?

- Meet with your academic advisor to understand the withdrawal process and financial impact, such as repayment of student loans.

- Lean on your support system of friends and mentors to help build and carry out your plan for the future.

Tip: Your plan should not include returning to your parent's basement to mooch off them forever.

Day 136

Secure a summer internship.

Finding a summer internship is a fantastic way to gain real-world experience. Start by exploring opportunities related to your interests or career goals. Check with your counselor, career center, or online job boards for listings. Contact local businesses, organizations, or alumni from your school who might offer know of opportunities. An internship gives you hands-on experience and helps you build a network of connections that could help you in the future. It also adds a competitive edge by demonstrating initiative and commitment to your chosen field. Even if the internship is unpaid, the experience and skills you gain are worth it.

Day 137

Try different study tactics until you find the best for you.

When it comes to studying, it's easy to fall into the trap of just reading over notes or highlighting textbooks, but active study methods can help lock in what you're learning. Instead of passively reviewing, try making flashcards or creating your own quizzes. Flashcards are like your personal memory boosters—they help you actively recall information, which is way more effective than just staring at a page. Writing your own quizzes tests your knowledge and makes you think about what's most important. It's like being both the student and the teacher, forcing your brain to engage with the material more deeply.

Day 138

Join a club with people who have similar interests.

Look for groups related to your hobbies, career goals, or passions: a debate team, art club, or environmental group, etc. By connecting with others who share your interests, you'll find a sense of community and belonging, making your transition to college smoother. Being active in clubs or organizations can also enhance your resume and provide valuable experiences that might be useful for future career opportunities. College is not just about academics; it's also about building a network and growing as a person. So, take the initiative to join a club, get involved, and make the most of your college experience.

Day 139

Don't tackle complex tasks when you're tired.

Your mind works best early in the day or right after a break, so use these peak times to dive into complex assignments or study sessions. Waiting until you're tired often leads to frustration and subpar work because your concentration and problem-solving skills diminish. By attacking demanding tasks when fresh, you set yourself up for success and avoid the stress of last-minute cramming or rushed efforts. Schedule challenging tasks during your high-energy periods and save more manageable, routine tasks for later. This approach not only improves the quality of your work but also helps manage stress and avoid burnout.

Day 140

Communicate with professors in an adult, respectful way.

Treat professors as professionals and address them politely, whether you're sending an email or speaking with them in person. Begin emails with a proper greeting and end with a courteous closing. Be clear and concise in your requests or questions and always use a formal tone. When meeting with professors, come prepared with specific topics or questions and respect their time. Understand that professors are there to support your learning, but they also appreciate professionalism and consideration.

Day 141

Take breaks while studying.

Trying to power through hours of nonstop studying might seem like a good idea, but it's not the most effective way to learn. Your brain can only focus for so long before it starts to feel like mush, and that's when everything you're reading starts to blur together. Instead, give your brain some breathing room. Study for 45-50 minutes, then take a 10–15-minute break. Get up, stretch, grab a snack, or take a short walk. This will help refresh your mind and make it easier to absorb the material when you get back to it. These short breaks also allow you to reflect on what you've just learned, which can help with retention. Plus, studying in chunks makes you more likely to stay motivated and avoid burnout.

Day 142

Take your time with a career or a major.

College is a time for exploration and self-discovery, and it's normal not to have everything figured out immediately. Permit yourself to explore different subjects and interests without fearing committing to a single path too soon. Take advantage of elective courses, join clubs related to various fields, and talk to professors and professionals to gain a broader perspective. Many students change their major at least once, and that's perfectly okay. It's more important to find what genuinely excites and motivates you than to settle on something to have a plan. Trust that with time and exploration, you'll discover what path is right for you. On the flip side, if you are super confident, don't second guess your choice.

Day 143

Ask questions during class and ask for clarification.

Asking questions is one of the best ways to ensure you get the material, not just memorize it. Your professors are there to help; they appreciate it when students are engaged and curious. If something doesn't make sense, raise your hand and ask for clarification. Perhaps someone else has the same question but is too shy to ask. Asking questions can also lead to deeper discussions and help you connect with your professors, which can be beneficial when you need recommendations or advice later. It's better to ask a question now than to struggle with the material later.

Day 144

Changing schools is rarely the solution.

Changing schools might seem like a quick fix to your problems, but it won't magically solve everything. While a new environment can offer fresh opportunities and perspectives, it's not a cure-all for your issues. Problems often follow you, no matter where you go, because they are about the place and how you handle them. Instead of focusing on a new school as the solution, address the challenges you face right where you are. Work on developing coping strategies, seeking support from friends, family, or counselors, and improving your problem-solving skills. Facing and overcoming obstacles can lead to personal growth and a better understanding of yourself. Focus on making the most of your current situation and building resilience, and you'll find yourself better equipped to handle challenges no matter where you are.

Day 145

Turn off your phone in class.

When your phone is on, even if it's silent, it's like having a constant pull on your attention. You might think you're just glancing at it for a second, but that second can turn into minutes, and before you know it, you've missed something important. Turning off your phone completely removes the temptation to check it, allowing you to fully engage with the material being taught. This small action shows respect for your education, professors, and classmates.

Day 146

There is a massive difference between getting an education and being educated.

Getting an education is about going to class, passing exams, and doing what's required to get that diploma. But being educated goes much further; it's developing a deeper understanding of the world and your place in it. It's about questioning what you're taught, seeking knowledge from different perspectives, and applying what you learn to real-life situations. An education gives you the tools, but knowing how to use them means being educated. College is your opportunity to do more than check boxes; it's your chance to grow intellectually and personally. So don't just aim to get an education—aim to be educated.

Day 147

Be sure to take a "just for fun" class every now and then.

College is the best time for exploration, and while it's important to focus on your major, it's also a chance to discover new passions. Maybe you've dabbled in photography, wanted to learn a new language, or have a secret interest in astronomy. Taking a class just because it sounds interesting can break up the monotony of your core courses and add some excitement to your schedule. Plus, it's a great way to meet new people outside your major who share similar interests. You might even uncover a hidden talent or find a new hobby that becomes a lifelong passion.

Day 148

Now's the time to separate yourself from what others expect and what you love to do.

It's easy to get caught up in what others expect of you, whether it's your parents, friends, or society. But now is the time to focus on what truly makes you happy and fulfilled. Explore different activities, take diverse classes, and dive into interests that excite you, even if they're not what everyone expects. Your college years are about self-discovery and growth, not just meeting others' expectations. Embrace this time to build a path that reflects your passions and strengths. This might mean pursuing a major you're passionate about rather than a safe choice or joining clubs that align with your interests, even if they're outside the mainstream.

Day 149

Courses fill up fast! Register for classes right away.

The last thing you want is to be stuck with a schedule full of classes that don't align with your major. Early registration gives you the best shot at getting the professors you want, the times that work best for you, and the classes that help you stay on track to graduate. It also means you'll avoid the stress of last-minute scrambles, where you might end up with an 8:00 a.m. class you didn't want or a course that's way out of your comfort zone just because it was the only one left. Don't procrastinate on this one—set a reminder, mark your calendar, and be ready to hit that registration button the moment it opens.

Day 150

Discipline is doing what needs to be done.

Discipline is all about pushing yourself to get things done, even when you'd rather be doing something else. Imagine you've got a pile of assignments and exams coming up, and you'd much rather binge-watch a show or hang out with friends. Discipline kicks in when you choose to hit the books instead, knowing that putting in the work now will pay off later. It's not always fun, but it's a crucial skill for success in college and beyond. It's normal to feel unmotivated at times, but that's when discipline really matters. It's the difference between reaching your potential and falling short.

Day 151

Consider a summer course to stay on track or get ahead.

A summer class can lighten your load during the regular semester, giving you more time to focus on challenging subjects or allowing for a more balanced schedule. Plus, it can help you catch up if you've fallen behind or want to knock out a requirement early. Summer courses often have smaller class sizes, meaning more one-on-one time with professors and a chance to dive deeper into the material. It's also a great way to explore a subject you're curious about without the pressure of a full course load. Whether you take the class on campus or online, you're making an investment in your future self. Enrolling in a summer course is a strategic step that can give you a serious advantage as you work toward your degree.

Day 152

Attend large lecture classes on subjects you're not taking.

Sitting in on large lecture classes for subjects you're not officially taking can be a fantastic way to explore new interests. Many colleges allow students to attend lectures outside their registered courses, offering a sneak peek into various fields of study. This approach helps you understand different subjects without committing to a full course load. It also lets you experience different teaching styles and see if a particular subject interests you. Attending these lectures can make you feel more connected to the academic community and inspire new areas of curiosity. Plus, it's a low-pressure way to explore topics that might not fit into your major but still fascinate you.

Day 153

Academic issues? Talk to your advisor.

Whether you're having trouble with a particular course, unsure about your major, or feeling overwhelmed by your workload, your advisor can help. They know the ins and outs of the system, from dropping a class to finding tutoring services, and they can help you create a plan to get back on track. Ignoring problems won't make them go away, and waiting too long can make things worse. They might suggest strategies you haven't considered or point you to resources you didn't know existed. College is a big transition, and asking for help is okay.

Day 154

Swap procrastination for planning.

Admit it, you procrastinate. We all do it! But, when you do, it only piles up stress and makes everything feel harder. Instead, make planning your new best friend. Start by breaking your tasks into smaller, manageable chunks and setting deadlines for each. Create a schedule or use a planner to keep track of your assignments, exams, and other commitments. When you plan, you avoid last-minute cramming and the panic of rushing to meet deadlines. Allocate specific times for studying, socializing, and downtime to create a balanced routine. Planning ahead also helps you spot potential issues before they become big problems, giving you time to adjust and seek help if needed.

Day 155

Take advantage of free tutoring by signing up early.

Sign up early to secure a spot and ensure you get the help you need before problems escalate. Tutors can provide valuable support, clarify difficult concepts, and help you develop effective study strategies. Waiting until the last minute often leads to added stress and limited availability, so being proactive is key. Many schools offer these services to help you succeed, so make it a priority to use them. Attending tutoring sessions regularly can keep you on track with your coursework and improve your understanding of challenging subjects. Remember, asking for help is a strength, not a weakness.

Day 156

Never ask the instructor, "Did I miss anything?"

This question can come off as arrogant because it puts the burden of catching you up on the instructor. Instead, take responsibility for your absence by reaching out to classmates to get notes and details on what content was covered. Review the syllabus and check if the instructor has posted any lecture materials online. If you still have questions after doing your leg work, then approach your instructor with specific questions about the material or assignments. This approach shows that you respect their time and are genuinely invested in learning.

Day 157

Take a public speaking class.

Speaking confidently and clearly is a skill that benefits you not only in class presentations but also in everyday interactions, job interviews, and your career. Public speaking classes teach you how to organize your thoughts, present them effectively, and handle the nerves that come with speaking in front of an audience. You will learn techniques for engaging listeners, using body language, and managing your pace and tone. These skills extend beyond the classroom, helping you lead group projects, participate in discussions, and make a strong impression in professional settings. Investing in your communication skills now will pay off in countless ways throughout your academic and professional life.

Day 158

Sit near the front of the class.

When you choose a seat close to the instructor, you can hear every word clearly and catch every detail of the lecture. This helps you stay focused and absorb the material more effectively. Sitting in the front row minimizes distractions, like chatting with classmates or the urge to check your phone, making it easier to engage with the lesson. Plus, being close to the front often means the professor is more likely to notice you, which can be helpful if you have questions or need additional support. Remember, your goal is to learn and succeed, so take control of your environment and use it to your advantage.

Day 159

Ask your professor how they got interested in their field.

When you take the initiative to learn about your professor, you connect on a more personal level and gain a deeper understanding of the subject matter. Professors often have fascinating stories about their path to academia, including pivotal moments, challenges they faced, and what motivates them. This conversation can also help you see the real-world applications of what you're studying and inspire you to explore the field further. Engaging with your professors in this way shows that you're genuinely interested in the subject and opens opportunities for mentorship and guidance, as professors are more likely to support students who actively engage with their work.

Day 160

Rewrite notes right after class while the material is fresh.

When you review your notes immediately, you reinforce what you just learned and fill in any gaps in your understanding. This habit helps solidify the concepts and makes studying later much easier. You can catch any mistakes or unclear points while the lecture is still fresh. This practice also prevents the pile-up of notes and reduces the stress of last-minute cramming before exams. Plus, keeping up with this routine can keep your study sessions more organized and effective. Aim to spend a few minutes after each class reviewing your notes and adding any details or clarifications.

Day 161

You are there to learn... not just pass exams.

While focusing solely on getting good grades is tempting, remember that the real goal is to absorb knowledge and develop skills. Treat each class as an opportunity to expand your understanding and think critically about the subject matter. Engage in discussions, ask questions, and dive into assignments with curiosity rather than just aiming for the highest grade. By immersing yourself in the material, you'll gain a deeper understanding and retain information better, serving you well beyond the classroom. Focus on mastering the concepts and connecting them to real-world applications.

Day 162

Take a challenging class and commit to getting an A.

College is the perfect opportunity to push yourself beyond your comfort zone and test your limits. Enroll in a course that sparks your interest or aligns with your goals, even if it feels intimidating. Embrace the challenge with a determined mindset and develop a plan to excel. The effort you invest will enhance your learning experience and build your confidence and resilience. Achieving an A in a tough class demonstrates your ability to tackle complex problems and succeed despite obstacles. It's a powerful way to highlight your dedication and potential.

Day 163

Service projects are great for hands-on learning.

Engaging in these projects allows you to apply what you've learned in real-world scenarios, giving you practical skills and insights you won't find in textbooks. Whether you're volunteering at a local nonprofit, participating in community clean-ups, or helping with a fundraising event, service projects teach you valuable lessons in teamwork, problem-solving, and leadership. You'll gain a deeper understanding of social issues and learn how to address them effectively, all while positively impacting your community. These experiences also help you build a strong resume and can even open doors for future internships or job opportunities. By getting involved in service projects, you develop a sense of responsibility and empathy while enhancing your college experience.

Day 164

Take advantage of mentor programs or become one.

Seek out a mentor who aligns with your goals and interests, whether through university programs, clubs, or professional networks. Their support can help you set and achieve goals, provide career insights, and connect you with opportunities. On the flip side, becoming a mentor offers a chance to give back, develop leadership skills, and gain a deeper understanding of your own experiences. Helping others can also broaden your perspective and strengthen your network. Engage in these programs with an open mind and a willingness to learn and teach.

Day 165

Talk to the professors in your major.

Your professors are knowledgeable about the subject matter and have insights into the field that can shape your academic and career path. They can advise on the best courses to take, recommend research opportunities, and provide guidance on internships or job prospects. Engaging with them builds connections that might lead to mentorship or valuable references later. Professors can also share their firsthand experiences and industry trends, giving you a clearer picture of what to expect and how to succeed. Don't wait until you're struggling or need something specific—make it a habit to reach out, ask questions, and seek feedback regularly.

Day 166

Take a few courses in your major as early as you can.

By diving into a few courses within your chosen major sooner rather than later, you allow yourself to explore whether the subject truly interests you or might not be the right fit. Starting early allows you to adjust your path without feeling like you're wasting time or credits. If you discover that a major isn't as exciting or suitable as you thought, you can pivot to a new direction with less stress. It also gives you a better understanding of what to expect in more advanced classes. If you find out the major isn't for you, that's okay! College is about discovering yourself and your interests.

Day 167

Stay on top of your reading material.

Falling behind on reading material can quickly spiral into a mountain of stress and missed deadlines. When you let readings pile up, you risk understanding the material poorly and struggling to catch up. Set aside dedicated time each day to tackle your reading list, breaking it into manageable sections. If you find yourself falling behind, address it immediately by prioritizing the most critical readings first and seeking help if needed. Reach out to classmates or your professor if you struggle to understand the material. Keeping pace with your readings helps you stay engaged in class discussions and grasp concepts more deeply. While using AI (Artificial Intelligence) programs to summarize material might be tempting, this will only give you a surface-level understanding.

Day 168

Don't assume instructors will make exceptions for you.

College is a time to develop responsibility and independence, and professors expect you to adhere to deadlines and guidelines. If you think you might need an extension or special consideration, address it early and communicate your situation honestly. Professors often have policies they must follow and may be unable to bend the rules for individual cases. It's important to understand that while instructors are there to support your learning, they also must balance fairness for all students. However, if you have a learning accommodation, be sure to meet with the office that handles educational assistance.

Tip: Respond politely if your request is denied. Getting angry or bashing your instructor is sure to backfire.

Day 169

Study at least three days before the exam, then rest.

Cramming the night before a big exam is not as effective as spreading out your study sessions and reviewing the content multiple times. Create a study schedule to break down the topics into manageable chunks and review each section thoroughly on different days. This approach helps reinforce your understanding and reduces stress. On the day before the exam, shift your focus to rest and relaxation. Avoid staying up late to cram; instead, review your notes briefly and then relax and give yourself time to unwind.

Day 170

The right study group can be priceless.

The right study group should mesh with your learning style and academic goals, offering support and diverse perspectives. Avoid groups where members are easily distracted or lack dedication. Discuss study habits and expectations upfront to ensure everyone is on the same page. A successful study group fosters collaboration, where everyone contributes and benefits from each other's strengths. If you're struggling to find a suitable group, consider starting your own group with friends or classmates who share similar academic objectives. Choose or create a group that keeps you on track and accountable, then regularly assess the group's dynamics and adjust if necessary.

Day 171

If you have a major term paper, don't procrastinate.

When faced with a major term paper, starting early. Begin by breaking down the paper into manageable sections, outlining your main points, and organizing your research. This initial step will help you visualize the structure of your paper and identify what information you need to gather. Spread your research over several weeks, allowing yourself to dive deep into each source. This approach reduces stress and ensures your paper is well-supported by solid evidence. By planning, you give yourself time to refine your thesis, develop coherent arguments, and revise your draft multiple times. This strategy will lead to a stronger, more polished paper.

Day 172

Take hard classes in the fall semester

Plan to take your harder classes in the fall semester—but maybe not during your first year. Fall offers the perfect setup for tackling challenging coursework. You're fresh off summer break, feeling more energized and focused, and ready to dive into new material. Professors also start the year with fresh enthusiasm, which can create a more engaging classroom experience. Plus, the fall semester tends to feel more focused overall, with fewer major distractions, compared to the spring, when thoughts of summer break can creep in and make it harder to concentrate.

Day 173

Teachers are the most helpful people you will ever know.

Teachers and professors have a wealth of knowledge and are often eager to assist students who show initiative. If you're struggling with a topic, reach out to your professor or teaching assistant for clarification. They can offer valuable insights, provide additional resources, and help you understand challenging material. Professors are used to students seeking help and are appreciative when they take an active role in their learning. Don't wait until you're overwhelmed; ask questions early and often. Building a relationship with your teachers can also lead to mentorship opportunities and valuable advice for your academic and career.

Day 174

Take advantage if notecards are permitted during exams.

Take full advantage if your professor allows note cards during an exam. Write down key concepts, formulas, and definitions that you find challenging. Use abbreviations and bullet points to maximize the space and make your notes easy to skim. Keep your notes neat and legible, as you'll need to be able to find information quickly. Practice using these cards while you study to get comfortable with the content and the layout. Refer to your cards strategically to clarify doubts or jog your memory on tricky topics. Note cards are a critical part of your exam strategy, so use them wisely.

Day 175

Recognize what comes easily to you because that's a hint as to what you were born to do.

Everyone has natural talents and skills that seem effortless, and these are often hints about your true calling. Pay attention to the activities or subjects where you excel without much struggle. If you find that understanding complex math problems feels intuitive, or if writing creative stories flows naturally, these are signals pointing you toward your strengths. Embrace these natural abilities and explore how they might shape your future career or academic path. The things that come easily to you often bring you joy and fulfillment, making them worth pursuing. They can guide you in choosing a major, selecting extracurricular activities, or even setting long-term career goals.

Day 176

When you lose all your excuses, you will find results.

It's easy to blame circumstances, distractions, or lack of time for falling short, but excuses only keep you stuck. Instead of letting excuses hold you back, face your challenges head-on. When you own up to your responsibilities and commit to your goals, you create opportunities for success. Start by setting clear, achievable objectives and breaking them into manageable tasks. Remove any barriers and embrace the hard work and discipline required to reach your goals. The more you focus on your actions rather than your reasons for not acting, the more you'll accomplish.

Day 177

Learn the material the first time it's presented.

When your professor introduces a new concept, focus on understanding it thoroughly right away. Pay attention to lectures, participate in discussions, and take detailed notes. If you find something confusing, tackle it immediately by asking questions, doing extra reading, or seeking help from classmates or tutors. By committing yourself to learning the material as it's taught, you'll reinforce your understanding and make studying for exams much easier. This habit also helps you stay on top of your coursework and prevents you from falling behind. It's not just about memorizing facts but truly grasping the concepts and their applications. This way, you build a solid foundation for more complex topics later.

Day 178

A double-major should align with your goals.

A double major can open more career opportunities and give you a competitive edge in the job market. Choose a practical major that aligns with your career goals and pair it with a complementary field that enhances your skill set. For example, combining a major in computer science with a minor in business can make you more versatile and attractive to employers. A focused double major helps you gain specialized knowledge and practical experience that can lead to better job prospects and higher earning potential.

Day 179

Find a good place to study outside of your living quarters.

Designate a quiet, distraction-free spot somewhere on campus where you can focus deeply and work efficiently. Libraries are ideal because they offer a calm environment and resources like books and study aids. Coffee shops or study lounges can provide a change of scenery and a bit of background noise, which might help you concentrate better, but they come with the potential for distraction. Choose a place that suits your study style—whether that's a space with whiteboards for brainstorming or a cozy corner for reading. By creating a study routine in a designated location, you signal to your brain that it's time to focus, which can boost your productivity. Plus, getting out of your living space helps you separate study time from relaxation time, making it easier to switch between work and leisure.

Day 180

If you can't explain it, you don't understand it well enough.

When you really understand something, you should be able to explain it, even to a friend who's never heard of it before. This isn't about dumbing things down; it's about making sense of what you're learning so deeply that you can turn a pile of jargon into something clear and easy to grasp. Imagine trying to explain a complicated topic from class to your grandma or a friend outside your major. If you stumble or get tangled up, that's a sign to dive deeper yourself. Professors and classmates who can really explain things aren't just smart, they know their stuff.

Day 181

Don't suffer in silence.

College can be overwhelming, and everyone faces challenges, but you don't have to handle them alone. Reach out for help when you need it. Start by talking to your professors or academic advisors, they're there to support you and can offer guidance or resources. Utilize campus support services like counseling centers or tutoring labs; these resources exist to help you succeed. Connect with classmates and friends; sometimes, just sharing what you're going through can make a big difference. Ignoring problems or keeping them to yourself can make things worse, so be open and communicate your needs. Your college experience is a time to learn and grow, both academically and personally.

Day 182

Read or skim material but do all the homework.

Reading or skimming the course material gives you a broad understanding of the topics, but real learning happens when you apply that knowledge through homework. Completing assignments helps reinforce what you've read, makes concepts clearer, and prepares you for exams. Homework often includes practice problems or critical thinking exercises that solidify your understanding and allow you to identify any gaps in your knowledge. It also gives you valuable feedback on how well you grasp the material. Make doing homework a priority and treat it as an opportunity to learn, not just a task to finish.

Day 183

"An investment in knowledge pays the best dividends."
— Benjamin Franklin

This quote means that putting your time and effort into learning is one of the smartest choices you can make. Think of your education as a long-term investment. Just like with money, the more you invest now, the greater the return you'll see later. Whether it's mastering a challenging subject or exploring a new area of interest, skills and insights you acquire will pay off in ways you might not immediately see. The effort you put into learning today will pay off far beyond your college years, helping you achieve your goals and realize your full potential.

Day 184

Don't feel stupid if you don't like what everyone else pretends to love.

College is a time when you'll encounter all sorts of trends and opinions, and it's easy to feel pressure to fit in. Embrace your own interests, even if they're different from what's trending. Whether it's a unique hobby, a specific type of music, or an unusual subject, your personal passions are what make you unique. Don't let the fear of judgment push you into pretending you're interested in something just to blend in. Authenticity is more valuable than conformity. People who are confident in their own likes and dislikes attract others who appreciate them for who they truly are. Focus on what genuinely excites you, and don't be afraid to explore your own path.

Here are a few responses you can keep handy:

- "It's not really my thing, but I can see why people love it."

- "I really appreciate the offer, but it's not the right fit for me."

- "Thank you for thinking of me, but I'm going to pass on this."

- "I've given it some thought, and I've decided to focus my time on other things."

Tip: A calm, confident tone and friendly smile goes a long way in keeping things respectful and kind.

Day 185

Read the entire syllabus for every class.

It might seem like just another piece of paper, but this document is your roadmap for the semester. The syllabus outlines everything you need to know about the course, from important dates and deadlines to the grading criteria and required materials. By reading it thoroughly, you get a clear picture of what's expected and how to succeed. You'll find out about major assignments, test dates, and even the professor's office hours. If you understand the syllabus from the start, you can plan your study schedule effectively and avoid last-minute surprises. It's also a great way to identify any potential conflicts or issues early on.

Day 186

Become an expert on course requirements and deadlines.

From the very beginning of each semester, take the time to thoroughly review the syllabus for every class. Mark important deadlines—like exams, essays, and projects—on a calendar or planner. Understand the grading criteria and what's expected in each assignment. If something's unclear, ask your professor for clarification right away. Staying on top of requirements shows you're serious about your education, and it will pay off in the long run. Remember, no one else is going to manage this for you, it's up to you to stay informed and be responsible for your academic journey.

Day 187

Professors like when you are truly interested in their class.

When you engage actively, ask thoughtful questions, and participate in discussions, you stand out as a dedicated learner. Professors notice students who come to office hours, seek additional resources, or bring up relevant topics related to the course. This enthusiasm not only helps you learn more but also builds a positive relationship with your professors. They're more likely to offer help, provide extra insights, or give you recommendations for future opportunities. Showing interest demonstrates that you value the subject matter and are committed to your education. Your genuine curiosity and active participation will be noticed and appreciated.

Day 188

Plagiarism is cheating. Period.

It's tempting to copy and paste or present someone else's work as your own, but don't fool yourself into thinking you'll get away with it. Colleges use sophisticated tools to detect plagiarism, and getting caught can have serious consequences, including failing the assignment or even being expelled. Always do your own work and give credit where it's due. Investing time in learning and creating your own ideas is better than risking your academic integrity for a shortcut. Stay honest and let your hard work and creativity shine. It's not worth compromising your future for a moment of convenience.

Day 189

Look into study abroad programs and keep an open mind.

College offers a unique opportunity to experience the world beyond your campus, and study abroad programs can be more accessible than you might think. Many schools offer scholarships, financial aid, and exchange programs to help cover the costs. Imagine studying history in Rome, practicing a new language in Spain, or exploring environmental science in Costa Rica. These experiences can expand your worldview, enrich your education, and make you stand out for future employers. Even if you're worried about finances, homesickness, or navigating a foreign country, remember that these challenges are part of adventure and growth. Some programs might last a summer, a semester, or even just a few weeks, so there's likely something that fits your schedule and budget. Keeping an open mind can lead to life-changing experiences that will shape your perspective and memories long after you graduate. Don't count yourself out before you've even investigated it, studying abroad might just be the highlight of your college journey.

Tip Taking general education classes when abroad can mean a lighter courseload and more time to enjoy the new culture.

Day 190

Attend the whole class, even if you don't feel like it.

It's tempting to skip out early or zone out, especially if you're tired, bored, or think you've heard it all before. But the truth is, you never know when something important will be covered—whether it's an unexpected tip for the exam, a clarification on a confusing concept, or just a nugget of wisdom that could change how you approach the subject. Professors often save key information for the end of the class, and you don't want to miss out. Even on those days when your bed or Netflix seems more appealing, push yourself to stay engaged for the entire class.

Day 191

Know what GPA is needed for a credit to count.

Different courses, majors, and institutions have varying standards, so don't assume that passing a class means you're in the clear. Some programs require a minimum GPA, often a 2.0 or 2.5, for credits to count toward your degree. For competitive majors or graduate school admissions, the bar can be even higher. If you don't meet these requirements, you might find yourself retaking classes or delaying graduation. Staying on top of your GPA isn't just about passing your classes; it's about ensuring your hard work pays off and gets you closer to your goals. Make it a habit to check your grades regularly and understand the specific GPA requirements for your major or program. Knowing what's at stake will motivate you to stay focused and keep your grades where they need to be.

Day 192

Be sure to answer exam questions in full.

Don't just skim the surface or give a quick response. Professors are looking for answers that demonstrate your understanding of the material. Even if the question seems straightforward, take the time to explain your reasoning, provide examples, and connect your answer to key concepts from the course. If a question has multiple parts, address each one fully. Leaving any part incomplete can cost you valuable points. Even if you're unsure about part of your answer, it's better to write something rather than leave it blank.

Day 193

Declare your major, then plan out all four years of classes.

Mapping out your coursework for the next few years can help you stay on track and ensure you meet all your graduation requirements. Start by reviewing the required and elective courses for your major and create a tentative schedule for each semester. This plan will allow you to balance challenging courses with lighter ones and fit in any internships, study abroad opportunities, or extracurricular activities you're interested in. Keep in mind that flexibility is key—sometimes course availability or personal interests might shift. Regularly check in with an academic advisor to adjust your plan as needed and to make sure you're on track.

Day 194

*www.ratemyprofessors.com can be helpful but
don't use that as the only criterion.*

Reviews on ratemyprofessors.com can be subjective and may not reflect your own learning style. Consider other factors like course content, professor qualifications, and how well the course aligns with your academic goals. Talking to classmates and seeking advice from academic advisors can provide a more comprehensive picture. Don't shy away from a professor because one person gave a bad review. But, if you hear the same negative feedback over and over again, you might want to think twice. Use multiple sources of information to make informed decisions about your professors and courses.

Tip: A tough professor might be what you need to excel.

Day 195

Be on time or early for class.

When you arrive to class early, you have time to settle in, review your notes, and get focused before the lecture starts. You're not rushing in, stressed out, or distracted, which means you're ready to absorb information right from the start. Plus, arriving early helps you snag a good seat where you can hear better, see the board clearly, and avoid distractions. Professors notice who consistently shows up on time, and that can leave a positive impression, especially if you ever need extra help or a recommendation letter.

Day 196

Set an academic goal by semester, by year, and overall.

Instead of wandering aimlessly through each semester, create clear, specific goals for what you want to achieve. Start by setting goals for each semester, like maintaining a certain GPA or mastering a challenging subject. Then, think bigger—what do you want to accomplish by the end of the year? Maybe it's making the Dean's List, landing an internship, or gaining a deeper understanding of your major. Finally, consider your overall goal for college. This could be graduating with honors, getting into a top graduate program, or being well-prepared for your career. These goals give you direction and help you stay focused.

Day 197

Never assume you know what was covered.

If you miss a class, don't just brush it off and assume you can catch up on your own. Every class session is packed with valuable information, discussions, and sometimes hints about what will be on the next exam. Missing out on that can put you at a serious disadvantage. The best move is to get notes from a reliable classmate as soon as possible. Even if you think you know what was covered, there's a good chance you missed something important. Falling behind, even a little, can snowball into bigger problems later. So, be proactive.

Day 198

---

*Criticism of your work is the professor's attempt
to bring out your potential.*

Professors provide feedback to push you beyond your comfort zone and help you improve. Their critiques are meant to challenge your thinking and refine your skills, not to attack your abilities or character. Approach criticism as a valuable tool for growth rather than a personal judgment. Embrace it as a chance to learn and enhance your work. Don't take it personally or get discouraged; instead, use it as motivation to better yourself and your assignments. Keep in mind that every successful student has faced criticism along their journey.

Day 199

Don't expect college to be the same as high school.

The challenges you faced in high school were just a warm-up. College brings more demanding coursework, stricter deadlines, and greater independence. Professors won't remind you about assignments. You're in the big leagues now and adjusting may take a full year. Be kind to yourself as you navigate this new level of expectation. Struggling initially doesn't mean you won't succeed— it's part of the process.

Day 200

A regular study time will help you stay focused.

When you stick to a consistent schedule, your brain gets used to the routine, making it easier to dive into study sessions without hesitation. Choose a time each day when you feel most alert and free from distractions and make it your dedicated study block. Whether it's early in the morning or late at night, find what works best for you and stick with it. This rhythm helps build discipline and makes studying a natural part of your day. Treat this time as a commitment, just like a class or a meeting, and guard it fiercely against interruptions. Over time, you'll find that this routine boosts your productivity, sharpens your focus and turns studying into a less daunting task.

Day 201

Get requirements out of the way early.

By tackling course requirements as soon as possible, you avoid the stress of last-minute scrambling and give yourself room to explore electives or dive deeper into your major later. Start by reviewing your degree plan and identifying all the required classes. Prioritize these courses in your first semesters to ensure you meet all the prerequisites and stay on track for graduation. You'll gain a solid foundation in essential subjects, which can make more advanced coursework easier to handle.

Day 202

Be open to new experiences, classes, and people.

Don't limit yourself to what you already know or what seems familiar. Dive into different subjects, even those outside your major, to discover new interests and talents. Attending events, joining clubs, and engaging with people from diverse backgrounds. Each new experience will broaden your perspective and enrich your college journey. Meeting people with different viewpoints can challenge your thinking and help you grow both personally and academically. Keep an open attitude toward the unexpected opportunities that come your way. Say yes to new classes, try out new activities, and connect with a variety of people.

Day 203

The hardest decisions are usually the most impactful.

Whether it's picking a major, deciding to study abroad, or balancing your workload, these decisions shape your future. Avoiding them might seem easier, but it can lead to missed opportunities and regret. Approach tough decisions with seriousness and an open mind. Weigh the pros and cons, seek advice from mentors, and reflect on what aligns with your long-term goals. Remember, growth happens outside your comfort zone.

Tip: Ask yourself, "Which choice aligns most with what I value or want for the future?"

Day 204

*"Educating the mind without educating the heart
is no education at all." — Aristotle*

Focusing solely on grades, tests, and academic achievements is easy, but remember that true education involves more than just intellectual growth. Developing empathy, compassion, and emotional intelligence is equally important. Strive to connect with others, understand different perspectives, and engage in meaningful conversations. Your college years offer countless opportunities to learn about yourself and others, so embrace them. Volunteer, participate in discussions, and build relationships with people from diverse backgrounds. Balancing your academic pursuits with efforts to grow emotionally will lead to a more fulfilling education.

Day 205

Pace yourself by spreading out difficult projects.

Breaking up major assignments and significant transitions into manageable chunks helps prevent overwhelming yourself and boosts your chances of success. This approach makes daunting tasks seem more doable and gives you time to review, adjust, and improve your work. Consistent effort is more effective than last-minute cramming or attempting too much at once. By pacing yourself, you'll reduce stress, maintain better focus, and achieve higher-quality results. Balancing your workload and allowing yourself breaks is essential for long-term success and well-being.

Chapter 4
Life Outside the Classroom: Navigating Clubs, Sports, and Social Scenes

Day 206

Give your family an advanced warning about significant physical and lifestyle changes.

Before heading home for a visit, give your family a heads-up about any significant changes, whether it's a new hair color, a nose ring, a tattoo, or even a new relationship. Sudden surprises can lead to awkwardness or misunderstandings, especially when the change is unexpected. If you're bringing a boyfriend or girlfriend home, let your family know in advance so they have time to process and prepare to welcome your guest. Likewise, a quick heads-up about visible changes can ease the situation and help everyone feel more comfortable. It's not about asking for permission but rather showing respect and consideration for their feelings while making personal choices that matter to you. Preparing them ahead of time can prevent uncomfortable reactions and keep the focus on enjoying your time together. A little communication goes a long way to create a positive and welcoming environment for your visit.

Day 207

True friends are people you feel safe with.

In college, you'll meet many people but finding friends who genuinely support and respect you is the key. These people listen without judgment, offer encouragement when needed, and stand by you through thick and thin. You should feel comfortable being yourself around them without the fear of criticism. True friends are also the ones who celebrate your successes and help lift you up during tough times. They respect your boundaries and are there to support you in the way you need, whether it's offering a listening ear, sharing a laugh, or simply being present.

Here are a few thoughtful ways to back out of a friendship:

- **The Gradual Fade**: "I've been really busy with personal priorities, so I won't be as available as before."

- **The Honest Conversation:** "I've appreciated our friendship, but I feel we've grown in different directions. I think it's best if we give each other some space."

- **Blame the Circumstances:** "Life's been pulling me in different directions, and I just don't have the capacity to keep up with everyone like I used to."

- **Setting Firm Boundaries:** "I'm focusing on my own well-being right now, and I need to step back from some relationships to do that."

Day 208

Your high school friendships will change.

It's normal for your high school friendships to change. It's not a sign that you're drifting apart or that your friendships are fading. Instead, it often means that everyone is settling into their new routines and embracing the excitement of their own college experiences. True friendships aren't defined by constant messaging or daily interactions. When you do catch up, it'll be like no time has passed. Cherish the moments you share and embrace the changes in your social life as part of growing up.

Day 209

Befriend other adults, not just your professors.

Staff members, such as academic advisors, librarians, cafeteria workers, and maintenance staff, are an incredible resource. These people keep the college running and often have tons of useful knowledge and experience to share. Academic advisors can help you navigate course selections and degree requirements, while librarians can assist with research projects and finding materials. The campus security team can offer safety tips and support, and the people working in the dining hall or student services can make your daily life a lot easier. These relationships can lead to valuable advice, networking opportunities, and even some behind-the-scenes perks. Plus, having a few friendly faces around campus is always good.

Day 210

Do not date within your dorm!

It might seem convenient to date someone who lives just down the hall, but it can lead to awkward situations if things don't work out. College dorms are already tight-knit environments and if a relationship goes south, you'll still have to see that person regularly. It can turn your living space into a source of tension, not just for you, but for everyone around you. Plus, dorm life is already full of drama—no need to add unnecessary complications to the mix. Focus on building friendships with the people you live with instead. If you want to date, expand your horizons outside the dorm, where it won't impact your day-to-day life as much. Keep your living situation stress-free and drama-free.

Day 211

True friends are not jealous of your other friendships.

True friends are those who support your other relationships and celebrate your connections with others. They understand that friendship is not a competition, but a way to enrich your life with diverse perspectives and experiences. When you have friends who are secure and supportive, they won't feel threatened or jealous when you spend time with others. Instead, they'll be happy for you and your growing circle of friends. True friends value your happiness and understand that building strong connections with a variety of people can enhance your life and will encourage you to nurture those relationships.

Day 212

Too much socializing can lead to bad grades.

When you're out partying or hanging out with friends constantly, it's easy to fall behind on assignments, miss study sessions, and neglect your coursework. Instead, prioritize your academic commitments by setting aside specific times for studying and completing assignments before diving into social events. It's about quality over quantity—choose social activities that enrich your experience and allow you to unwind without compromising your academic performance. Being disciplined about your study habits and knowing when to say no to social invitations can help you achieve the right balance. In the end, finding this equilibrium will ensure that you make the most of your college experience and help you achieve your academic goals.

Day 213

Never leave a drink unattended.

Leaving your drink unattended at a party, even briefly, can create an opportunity for someone to tamper with it, leading to potential drugging or contamination. To stay safe, always keep your drink with you, and if you need to step away, finish it first or get a fresh one when you return. In addition to watching out for your safety, keep an eye on your friends. Trust your instincts—if something feels wrong or you suspect your drink might have been tampered with, don't risk it.

Day 214

Keep in touch with your siblings.

As you dive into your new routine, balancing classes, social activities, and possibly part-time jobs, losing touch with family is easy. But remember, your siblings have been a significant part of your life and can offer support and perspective that's uniquely valuable. Regularly check in with them through calls, texts, or even video chats. Sharing your college experiences, both high and low, helps maintain your bond and provides a sense of continuity amidst the changes. Your siblings can be your biggest cheerleaders and a source of comfort when things get tough, because they understand who you are outside of college life.

Day 215

Don't let falling in love define your college experience.

Relationships can be incredibly rewarding but can also become all-consuming if you're not careful. Make sure you balance your relationship with your other responsibilities and opportunities. Embrace the chance to learn about yourself and the world around you, independent of your relationship. It's essential to maintain your own interests and goals and not let a relationship overshadow the broader college experience. While sharing your journey with someone special is great, ensure you're still making the most of all the opportunities college offers. Love can be a wonderful part of your college experience, but it should complement, not dominate, your time at school.

Day 216

Don't let FOMO get the best of you.

The fear of missing out (FOMO) is real in college, and it can sneak up on you fast. There's always something happening—parties, events, clubs, random late-night hangouts—and it's easy to feel like you have to do it all or you'll miss out. But here's the thing: trying to be everywhere all the time will wear you out. You don't need to say yes to everything just because everyone else is going. It's totally fine to skip stuff, chill in your room, or do your own thing. Your time and energy are valuable, and you'll enjoy college way more if you focus on what actually matters to you. Some of the best memories come from spontaneous moments with people you vibe with, not from forcing yourself to show up just to "be there." So don't stress about missing an event—there will always be another.

Day 217

Be nice to geeks; you'll probably end up working for one.

In college, you'll cross paths with all kinds of people, and some of them might come across as "geeks" or "nerds." The truth is that many of these so-called "geeks" will grow up to be experts in their fields and leaders in their industries. Imagine the future: you might find yourself working for one of these brilliant minds or needing their expertise on a project. Building a network of supportive, talented people can open doors you didn't even know existed. Embrace diversity and recognize each person's value. Today's "geek" could be tomorrow's industry game-changer.

Day 218

Get sporting event tickets when they are first available.

Football and basketball tickets often sell out quickly, especially for popular games, and buying them early ensures you won't miss out. Even if you decide later that you can't attend the game, you can usually sell the tickets later. Having tickets in hand gives you flexibility and the chance to benefit from high demand if you need to sell them. Securing your tickets early means you can plan and enjoy the excitement of the game without stress.

Day 219

The less you respond to negative people, the more peaceful your life will become.

Engaging with or responding to negative people is tempting, but doing so can drain your energy and disrupt your peace. Instead, focus on preserving your own well-being by choosing not to react to negativity. When you ignore the complaints and drama of others, you protect your mental space and maintain a more positive outlook. You can't control how people act, but you can control how you respond to them. Minimizing your interactions with those who spread negativity creates room for more constructive and uplifting experiences. Surround yourself with supportive, positive individuals who inspire and motivate you. When you let go of the need to engage with every negative comment or situation, you'll find that your life becomes quieter, more peaceful, and more aligned with your personal aspirations.

Day 220

Spend time with people who have different viewpoints.

When you surround yourself with individuals who think differently, you gain new insights and learn to see issues from various angles. This practice enriches your college experience and prepares you for real-world interactions where diverse viewpoints are common. Even if you disagree, listening to others' opinions fosters critical thinking and helps you develop stronger, more nuanced arguments. It also builds empathy, as you understand why people hold certain beliefs and how their experiences shape their views. So, seek out conversations and connections with those who challenge your thinking. It may feel uncomfortable at times, but this discomfort often leads to personal growth and an open-minded outlook.

Day 221

Embrace differences.

When you encounter someone with a different background, perspective, or way of thinking, see it as an opportunity to grow. Instead of sticking to familiar comfort zones, challenge yourself to understand their viewpoint and experiences. Approach these interactions with curiosity and an open mind. Ask questions, listen actively, and reflect on what new perspectives you can gain.

Tip: An easy way to engage someone is to ask, "I'm intrigued. Can you help me understand your experience?"

Day 222

Don't hang out with big spenders.

When you surround yourself with friends who regularly splurge on expensive items or lavish activities, you might feel pressured to keep up and spend more than you can afford. It's easy to get caught up in the excitement of shopping sprees or high-priced outings, especially if they seem like the norm in your social circle. Instead, build relationships with people who share your values about saving and budgeting. Choose friends who appreciate thoughtful spending and prioritize financial responsibility. It's okay to have fun and enjoy activities, but doing so within your means ensures that you don't overspend and end up stressed about money.

Day 223

Don't be afraid to switch friends.

College is a time for growth and self-discovery, and sometimes that means reevaluating your friendships. If you find that certain friends are dragging you down, encouraging unhealthy habits, or simply not aligning with the person you're becoming, it's okay to distance yourself. Building a supportive and positive social circle is crucial for your well-being and success. Seek out friends who inspire you, share your values, and contribute positively to your life. It might be uncomfortable at first to make new connections or let go of old ones, but remember, quality matters more than quantity. Surround yourself with people who challenge you in good ways, support your goals, and make you feel valued.

Day 224

Carrying condoms is not as awkward as an unexpected pregnancy.

Having condoms on hand is a responsibility that can help you avoid serious situations and keep you in control of your health and future. Think of it as a proactive step toward being prepared rather than facing an unplanned and potentially life-altering challenge later. It's much easier to handle the small inconvenience of carrying condoms than the much bigger issue of unplanned parenthood or disease. Taking care of your sexual health is just as important as any other part of your college experience. By being prepared, you show that you're taking charge of your well-being and making thoughtful choices for your future. So, don't let embarrassment hold you back.

Day 225

Never try to be the smartest person in the room.

Surrounding yourself with individuals who possess more knowledge or different perspectives encourages personal growth and continuous learning. You stay motivated and intellectually stimulated when you're constantly engaged with those who push your boundaries. Getting comfortable is easy when you're the top dog, but real progress happens when pushed beyond your comfort zone. Seek out people who bring fresh ideas, diverse viewpoints, and expert knowledge. Growth often comes from being around those who know more than you do.

Day 226

Don't talk about people behind their backs.

When you gossip about someone, you risk damaging your reputation and jeopardizing your relationships with others. Instead, focus on addressing issues directly with the person involved or keeping your thoughts to yourself. Maintaining respect and integrity in your conversations will build trust and help you avoid unnecessary drama. Refusing to talk behind others' backs creates an environment where people feel valued and trusted. This approach enhances your personal relationships and sets a positive example for those around you.

Day 227

Spend time with people who lift you up, not tear you down.

Look for friends who encourage your goals, celebrate successes, and support you during tough times. Being around positive people helps you stay motivated and confident and contributes to a healthier, happier college life. On the other hand, those who criticize, undermine, or create drama can drain your energy and affect your self-esteem. Recognize the value of nurturing relationships that inspire and empower you. Invest in friendships that make you feel good about yourself and help you grow. By surrounding yourself with uplifting and supportive people, you build a strong network that enhances your college experience and personal growth.

Day 228

Listen to people who encourage you to do what is right.

Instead of following orders from people who try to dictate your path, focus on listening to those who genuinely encourage you to follow your instincts. Trust yourself and your inner voice, because it often knows what's best for you. Pay attention to advice from people who support your dreams and goals and help you stay true to your values. These are the people who believe in your potential and want to see you succeed on your own terms. When you stay aligned with your sense of purpose and make decisions based on what feels right for you, you'll find more satisfaction and fulfillment in your journey.

Day 229

When going on a date, make sure someone knows where you're going and with whom.

Before you head out on a date, text a friend or family member with details about your date, including the location, time, and who you'll be meeting. If your plans change or you need to stay out longer, keep them updated. This practice helps ensure your safety and provides backup if things don't go as planned. It's better to be prepared and have someone aware of your whereabouts, just in case you need help or there's an unexpected situation. Also, choosing a public place for your dates is a good idea, especially when meeting someone for the first time.

Day 230

Success largely depends on working with people.

College isn't just about solo study sessions or acing exams; it's a social environment where teamwork and communication play a crucial role. Group projects, study groups, and campus activities require you to work alongside diverse individuals, each with their own perspectives and strengths. Building strong relationships with classmates, professors, and peers can open doors to new opportunities, enhance your learning experience, and help you navigate challenges more efficiently. Practice being a good listener, show respect for others' ideas, and constructively contribute your insights. These skills help you in academic settings and prepare you for future professional environments where teamwork and collaboration are essential.

Day 231

Surround yourself with those who bring out the best in you.

Genuine friends will support you, celebrate your successes, and help you through challenges. They will uplift you rather than drag you down. Choose friends who share your values, interests, and goals and who make you feel good about yourself. Avoid those who only bring drama or pressure you into negative behaviors. Building a circle of supportive, positive friends will make your college experience more rewarding and enjoyable. Quality matters more than quantity when it comes to friendships.

Day 232

Create a strong network.

College is a prime time to meet people who can help shape your future, so don't shy away from introducing yourself and sharing your goals. Let people know who you are and what you're passionate about. Your next opportunity or valuable connection might be just one "Hello" away. Being approachable and expressing your interests clearly opens doors to unexpected opportunities and collaborations. Whether it's a professor who can offer career advice, or a guest speaker who inspires you, every interaction is a chance to build your network. Networking isn't just about getting something; it's about creating genuine relationships and offering help in return. Keep in touch with those you meet and build meaningful connections over time. The more people you know, the more opportunities become available to you.

Day 233

Make friends with good-hearted people.

Good-hearted friends offer a sense of community and trust that makes navigating college life more enjoyable and less stressful. These friendships will enrich your college experience, providing a solid support system and making your journey more fulfilling. Avoid those who might bring negativity or drama into your life; they can drain your energy and derail your goals. The quality of your friendships often impacts your overall college experience, so choose wisely and nurture those bonds.

Day 234

In relationships, don't lose yourself.

College will bring many new experiences and relationships, and while it's natural to grow and evolve, don't let your identity get lost in someone else's expectations or desires. Maintain your own interests, passions, and goals, even as you build connections with others. It's easy to get caught up in trying to please someone or adapting too much to fit into a relationship, but this can lead to losing sight of your own needs and values. Balance is key. Ensure you're investing in yourself, pursuing your hobbies, and focusing on your personal goals. Healthy relationships should support and enrich your life, not overshadow it. If you compromise too much or feel like you're changing who you are to fit in, it might be time to reassess the relationship.

Day 235

Your parents are excited too.

Your parents are just as excited as you are, and they'll want to hear about your experiences. They're not just asking out of curiosity; they genuinely care and are eager to share in your journey. Keep them in the loop by sharing details about your daily life and even the small things that make you smile. It's a great way to stay connected and show appreciation for their support. Sharing these experiences helps them feel involved and reassured, knowing that you're adjusting well. Your parents will appreciate the effort.

Day 236

Be kind to unkind people, as they usually need it the most.

In college, you'll encounter a mix of personalities, including some who might seem unkind. While reacting with frustration or indifference is tempting, remember that unkindness often stems from personal struggles or insecurities. By choosing to be kind to those who might not treat you well, you offer them a glimpse of empathy and compassion they might be missing. Your kindness can act as a bridge, breaking down barriers and potentially transforming someone's behavior. Being kind to unkind people doesn't mean you have to tolerate bad behavior to become besties, but it does mean that you approach the situation with understanding rather than hostility.

Day 237

You don't have to drink yourself stupid to have fun.

Having fun doesn't mean you need to overdo it with alcohol to enjoy yourself. It's easy to think that everyone is drinking excessively, but that's not the case. When you stay in control, you can truly enjoy the moment, make better memories, and avoid the regrettable decisions that often come with drinking too much. Plus, you won't have to deal with nasty hangovers, embarrassing stories, or worse yet, pictures on the internet!

Day 238

Try to make at least one friend in every class.

It might feel intimidating at first but having at least one person you can count on makes a huge difference. A friend in class can be a study buddy, someone to share notes with, or even just someone to chat with before the lecture starts. Connecting with people makes you more likely to stay engaged and motivated. Don't worry if you're not naturally outgoing; a simple "Hey, how's it going?" can go a long way. These friendships can also grow beyond the classroom, leading to a more connected college experience overall. That one classmate could turn into a lifelong friend.

Day 239

People can fool you.

Not everyone you meet will have your best interests at heart. Some people might put on a friendly face but have hidden agendas, while others might seem trustworthy but disappoint you when it matters most. This doesn't mean you should be paranoid or overly suspicious, but it's wise to be cautious and not take everyone at face value. Pay attention to actions more than words—people can say anything, but their behavior will reveal their true character over time. Trust your instincts; if something feels off, it probably is. It's okay to take your time to really get to know someone before letting them into your inner circle. College is full of new experiences and people, and while it's exciting, it's also a time when you must protect yourself from being misled.

Day 240

Step away from Twitter, Tik Tok and Instagram

Doom scrolling through endless posts, watching short clips, and comparing yourself to others can become a habit that eats up hours without you even realizing it. But college is your time to build real connections and live in the moment. Instead of watching someone else's life online, focus on making your own life exciting and fulfilling. You'll find that the world beyond your screen is full of opportunities that are way more rewarding than any number of likes or follows. Added bonus! Stepping away from social media will help you avoid the trap of comparing yourself to others, which can drain your confidence and happiness.

Day 241

Roommate issues? Talk to your RA first.

If you're dealing with roommate issues, don't let them fester. Your RA can offer advice, mediate a conversation between you and your roommate, and even help you come up with a compromise that works for both of you. Avoid making things worse by sending passive-aggressive text messages or stewing in silence. Instead, approach your RA with a clear idea of what's bothering you and what you'd like to see change. They've seen it all before and have the experience to guide you toward a solution.

Day 242

Always have a buddy when walking on campus at night.

Campus environments can be large and sometimes isolated after dark, so having someone with you is smart. If you don't have a friend available, many colleges offer escort services or campus security that can provide safe transport to your destination. Trust your instincts: if something feels off, avoid walking alone, and seek assistance. By sticking together, you protect yourself and contribute to a more secure environment for everyone on campus.

Day 243

Date, but don't get serious too soon.

Dating in college can be a lot of fun, but don't rush into anything too serious. This time in your life is all about exploring who you are, meeting new people, and figuring out what you want. If you dive into a serious relationship right away, you might miss out on experiences that could help you grow as a person. Keep things light and focus on getting to know different people. That way, you can figure out what you really want in a partner without feeling tied down. Plus, college is a time when people change a lot, and what you want now might be different from what you want later. Give yourself the space to grow, both individually and in your relationships. If something starts to feel too intense or like it's taking over your life, it's okay to step back. Remember, there's no rush. You've got time to enjoy the dating scene and figure things out at your own pace.

Day 244

Not everyone drinks their way through college.

Despite what you might think, plenty of students choose not to drink and still have a great time. In fact, staying sober can help you make better decisions, stay focused on your goals, and avoid the regret that often comes with overdoing it. You'll also be more in control of your time and energy, which means you can take full advantage of everything college has to offer. Don't feel pressured to drink just because it seems like everyone else is doing it. The reality is that lots of students are making the same choice to stay sober, and they're doing just fine. You can too. College is what you make of it, and you have the power to create the experience you want, with or without alcohol.

Day 245

Never accept a drink from someone you don't know.

Accepting a drink from a stranger can put you at risk of being drugged or drinking something you didn't expect, leading to dangerous situations. It's not worth the risk, even if you're trying to be polite or think it's just a harmless gesture. Always be in control of what you're drinking. If you didn't see it poured or open it yourself, it's best to decline. If you're out with friends, watch out for each other and make sure everyone stays safe. It's easy to let your guard down in the excitement of college life, but your safety is far more important than any temporary fun.

Day 246

Most people do not marry their college sweetheart.

It's easy to get swept up in the excitement of a new romance and think you've found "the one," but college is a time for exploring who you are and what you want out of life. Your feelings and goals might change as you grow and experience new things. Instead of locking yourself into the idea that your first college relationship must be your last, focus on learning from each person you meet. Enjoy the time you spend together, but don't let it limit your opportunities or experiences. Remember that relationships in college can be intense and full of learning moments, but they're not always forever. Don't be afraid to let go if something isn't working out; it's okay to grow apart and move on.

Day 247

Make holiday travel plans early for the best rates.

Don't wait until the last minute, thinking you'll find a better deal—prices usually go up the closer you get to the holidays. By planning, you can relax knowing your trip is locked in and you won't be stuck with overpriced tickets or inconvenient layovers. Set a reminder on your phone to start looking for tickets as soon as you know your holiday schedule. If you have a flexible schedule, you might even find cheaper rates by traveling a day or two before or after the peak travel days. Don't forget to check for student discounts, which can sometimes save you even more.

Day 248

Maturity is when someone hurts you and you try to understand their situation instead of hurting them back.

When someone wrongs you, take a step back and consider why they might have acted that way. Maybe they are dealing with their own issues or pressures that you're unaware of. By approaching the situation with empathy and an open mind, you not only prevent further escalation but also demonstrate emotional intelligence and self-control. This mature response can lead to a more constructive resolution and often helps to mend relationships. Reacting with kindness and understanding in the face of adversity reflects your personal growth and sets a positive example for those around you.

Day 249

Look for non-destructive ways to have fun.

Instead of turning to risky or destructive behaviors, explore creative and safe options for having fun. Try organizing a game night with friends, attending campus events, or joining clubs that match your interests. Outdoor activities like hiking or biking are great ways to unwind and have a blast without any negative consequences. If you're into art, go to a local art gallery or dive into projects or workshops that let you express yourself. Engaging in these kinds of activities keeps things fun and helps you build positive habits and relationships. Remember, the best memories are often made when you're simply enjoying the moment and being yourself.

Day 250

Only bring cash when you go out to limit spending.

Carrying cash instead of credit or debit cards can be a powerful way to control your expenses and stick to your budget. When you use cash, you can physically see how much money you have left, making it easier to manage your spending and avoid impulse purchases. Set a specific amount of cash for each outing, and once it's gone, resist the urge to spend more. Keeping the cards at home also ensures you won't misplace them or leave them behind.

Day 251

Long-distance relationships suck.

Long-distance relationships can be incredibly challenging and often come with more headaches than they're worth. They test your patience and commitment in ways you might not expect. You're separated by miles, and communication can feel like a constant juggling act between different time zones and schedules. The lack of physical presence means missing out on spontaneous moments and everyday interactions that strengthen connections. While some people manage to make long-distance relationships work, they require extra effort, trust, and frequent communication to keep the bond strong. If you find yourself in a long-distance situation, be prepared for the emotional ups and downs that come with it. It might be worth re-evaluating if the relationship is truly worth the stress or if it's better to focus on building more immediate and fulfilling connections.

Day 252

Just because you were friends at home doesn't mean you'll be BFFs in college.

College life is a whole new adventure with new experiences, environments, and people. As you dive into different classes, join new clubs, and meet a variety of people, your interests and daily routines will likely shift. This can create a natural distance between old friends who might be pursuing different paths or developing new priorities. Don't be surprised if you find yourself drifting apart from friends you once thought you'd stay close to forever. Embrace the opportunity to make new connections and discover who you are outside of your old friend group. It's perfectly okay to let some friendships evolve or even fade as you grow.

Day 253

Cover your drinks. Cover yourself. Eat healthily.

When you go out, always cover your drink to protect it from potential tampering. Similarly, prioritize protection by using condoms to safeguard both yourself and your partner. Beyond safety, focus on your overall well-being by eating healthily. Good food fuels your body and mind, keeping you energized and focused. Eating nutritious foods supports your academic performance, boosts your mood, and helps you manage stress better. These simple steps are not about being overly cautious but about making smart choices to protect your health and safety.

Day 254

Clubs and activities should be fun, not stressful.

Clubs and activities in college should enhance your experience, not add stress. Choose ones that genuinely interest you and bring joy rather than those that feel like an obligation. When you join a club or activity, remember it's about balancing fun with involvement. If a particular group or event starts feeling overwhelming, reassess your commitment. It's okay to step back if it begins to affect your well-being or academic performance. Prioritize quality over quantity—being deeply engaged in a few activities you love is more fulfilling than spreading yourself too thin across many.

Day 255

Don't let a little dispute injure a great friendship.

Conflicts are a natural part of any relationship, but they don't have to break the bond you've built. When disagreements arise, approach them with an open mind and a willingness to understand the other person's perspective. Communicate openly and calmly and focus on finding a resolution rather than winning the argument. Maintaining a great friendship often means being willing to forgive and move on. If you let minor disputes fester, they can turn into bigger issues that overshadow the positive aspects of your friendship. Instead, address problems directly and work through them together. True friends will appreciate your effort to resolve conflicts and value your friendship even more.

Day 256

The most important thing for success is knowing how to get along with people.

Building strong relationships is key, whether you're working on a group project, participating in campus activities, or interacting with professors and classmates. Show respect, listen actively, and be genuinely interested in others' ideas and perspectives. Understanding and adapting to different personalities will help you navigate social dynamics smoothly. Practice empathy and be supportive, offering help when needed and celebrating others' successes. By encouraging positive interactions and avoiding unnecessary conflicts, you create a network of people who will support and lift you up.

Day 257

A few minutes of sex is not worth years of regret.

Before jumping into a physical relationship, think carefully about the potential consequences. Make sure you're fully ready and comfortable with your choices, and consider the impact on your emotional well-being, health, and future relationships. Understand the risks involved, including unintended pregnancies and sexually transmitted diseases, and take necessary precautions. It's important to remember that sex should be a consensual, respectful, and meaningful part of a relationship, not a decision driven by pressure or impulse. You can avoid situations that lead to long-term regret by staying in control of your choices.

Day 258

You may not know where you fit, but someone's life may never be complete without you.

Each interaction you have, no matter how small, contributes to the larger picture of your experience. Don't underestimate the impact you can have simply by being yourself and showing kindness. Whether you're a friend, a classmate, or a mentor, your unique qualities and actions help shape others' lives in meaningful ways. Embrace this idea with openness and confidence, knowing that your contributions, however modest, are valuable. Keep being genuine, supportive, and engaged; you might be the piece someone else needs to feel complete. Even if you never fully understand your role, trust that your presence and efforts are shaping the lives of those around you in ways that you may never fully see.

Day 259

Learn to leave relationships if you feel small and insecure.

If you find yourself constantly feeling belittled or unworthy, it's a clear sign that a friendship or relationship may not be healthy. Respect yourself enough to step away from connections that drain your energy or undermine your self-esteem. Doing so creates space for positive, affirming relationships that help you grow. It's not selfish to prioritize your well-being; it's a necessary part of creating a supportive environment for personal development. As you move forward, focus on building connections with people who bring out the best in you and encourage you to reach your full potential.

Day 260

Your loved ones miss you more than you know.

As you embrace your college experience, remember that a simple phone call or text can mean the world to your loved ones. Your parents and siblings are adjusting to your absence and think about you often, wishing they could be a part of your new adventures. It doesn't hurt to reach out and share a bit of your life with them. A quick update or a friendly chat can bridge the gap between home and college, and it's a great way to keep them in the loop about your experiences. They're your biggest supporters, and hearing from you can lift their spirits as much as it lifts yours. Even if you're busy, taking a few minutes to connect can strengthen your relationship and remind you of your strong support system back home.

Day 261

Don't take a stranger's comments personally.

People can be real jerks in high school, and guess what? You'll find some of those same people in college, too. If someone treats you poorly or rudely, remember it's not necessarily about you. Often, people act out because of their own issues or insecurities, and if they don't know you personally, their behavior says more about them than it does about you. Don't let their negativity get under your skin. Focus on building genuine connections with people who appreciate you for who you are. Brush it off when you encounter those who try to drag you into drama or make you feel bad

Day 262

You don't have to agree with everyone's opinions.

You don't have to agree with everyone you meet, but listening to and respecting their views is important. Just as you want others to hear you out and value your perspective, you should do the same for them. Embracing diverse opinions means engaging in conversations, even when you don't share the same viewpoint. It helps you grow, understand different perspectives, and build meaningful connections. When you find yourself in a discussion where opinions clash, approach it with an open mind and a respectful attitude. You might not change your stance, but you'll gain insight into why others think the way they do. Respectful dialogue fosters a positive environment and helps you develop the social skills needed for personal and professional relationships.

Day 263

Time will reveal who's there for you.

Building a wide circle of friends allows you to explore different perspectives, interests, and social dynamics. At first, it might seem overwhelming but don't stress. Time will naturally sort out who truly supports and values you. Some friendships will grow stronger, while others might fade away. That's part of the process. The goal isn't just to have a lot of friends but to find meaningful connections. By the end of your college journey, you'll have a clearer picture of who is truly there for you and who was passing through.

Day 264

A serious relationship may cause your grades to suffer.

College demands a lot of time and energy, and a deep relationship can quickly become a major focus. When you're emotionally invested, letting other priorities slip is easy. You might find yourself distracted during study sessions, missing deadlines, or struggling with coursework. Balance is essential, and while a relationship can be a wonderful aspect of your life, it shouldn't overshadow your academic responsibilities. If you find yourself overwhelmed, it's okay to take a step back and reassess how to balance your relationship with your studies. Keep open communication with your partner about your academic commitments and work together to support each other's goals.

Day 265

Keep your friends and drinks in sight at parties.

Parties can be lively and distracting, so losing track of things is easy. To stay safe, ensure your friends are within sight so you can support each other and look out for potential issues. If you need to step away from your drink, finish it or get a new one to avoid tampering. It's important to stay aware of your surroundings and not leave your drink unattended, as this can put you at risk. Leaving your phone or purse unattended is a recipe for disaster. By staying vigilant and ensuring you and your friends are accounted for, you can enjoy the party while prioritizing safety.

Day 266

Compliments are a fantastic way to start a conversation.

People naturally appreciate positive feedback; a sincere compliment can break the ice and make you and the other person feel more at ease. Let them know when you notice something you like about the other person, whether it's their style, smile, or enthusiasm. For example, you might say, "I really like your shoes," or "Your presentation was fantastic; you made the topic so interesting." Compliments create a friendly atmosphere and show that you're observant and engaged. They open the door to further conversation by giving the other person something to talk about or a topic to expand on.

Day 267

Be careful who you trust: sugar and salt look the same.

Just as sugar and salt look alike but taste completely different, people can present themselves one way but have very different intentions. As you start college, you'll meet a lot of new faces, and it's important to be cautious about who you let into your inner circle. Take time to get to know people before sharing personal information or relying on them for support. Watch how they act in different situations and how they treat others. Trust should be earned through consistent actions and genuine behavior, not just initial appearances. Use your instincts and judgment when evaluating who to trust and keep your guard up until you're sure someone has proven their reliability and integrity.

Chapter 5
*More Than a Major: Turning Passion
Into Purpose*

Day 268

---

*Even if your dream company is not hiring, you can still
reach out as a prospective employee.*

Expressing interest in a company you admire can set you apart from others even when they're not actively recruiting. Start by thoroughly researching the company to understand its culture, values, and recent developments. Craft a thoughtful and personalized message highlighting your admiration for their work and explaining how your skills and experiences align with their goals. Attach a well-prepared resume and a tailored cover letter and suggest ways you could contribute to their team. This proactive approach shows initiative and enthusiasm, which can leave a positive impression. Even if a position isn't available right now, you might be considered for future opportunities or networking connections. Many companies appreciate proactive and passionate candidates and may keep your information on file for future openings.

Day 269

Read the entire lease before signing.

Before you commit, thoroughly reviewing the lease agreement for any apartment or house is crucial. This document outlines your rights and responsibilities as a tenant, and understanding every detail can prevent future headaches or legal issues. Pay attention to clauses about penalties for breaking the lease early or any fees for overdue payments. Make sure you know your obligations and the landlord's responsibilities. Don't hesitate to ask questions or seek clarification before signing if anything is unclear or unfair. Remember, a lease is a legally binding contract and knowing what you're agreeing to can save you from potential disputes and financial surprises.

Day 270

Learn to make the best of how things turn out.

Life rarely goes exactly as planned, and unexpected challenges are inevitable. However, how you respond to these situations can make all the difference. Instead of focusing on what went wrong or what you didn't get, shift your focus to making the most of the circumstances you're given. This can remind you that a positive attitude and proactive approach can significantly impact your success and happiness. Adapt, find solutions, and keep moving forward with a positive mindset. Life is not just about waiting for things to improve but actively working to make the best of every situation.

Day 271

Decide what you want, then work on it every day.

Clarifying your goals is the first step toward achieving them. By defining what you want and putting it in writing, you create a tangible target to aim for. Craft a detailed plan outlining the steps you need to take to reach your goals, breaking it down into manageable tasks. Once you have your plan, commit to taking consistent action. Dedicate time each day to work towards your objectives, no matter how small the steps may seem. Daily effort builds momentum and keeps you on track. Regularly review your progress and adjust your plan as needed to stay aligned with your goals. This disciplined approach turns your ambitions into reality, helping you stay focused and motivated. Even with a plan, prepare for unexpected opportunities and pivot if it makes sense.

Day 272

Establish an emergency fund as soon as possible.

An emergency fund provides a safety net in case of unexpected expenses, such as medical emergencies, car repairs, or job loss. Calculate your essential monthly expenses, including rent, utilities, food, and transportation. Aim to save enough to cover these costs for at least six months. Begin by setting aside a small amount from each paycheck and gradually increase your savings as you can. Keep your emergency fund in a separate, easily accessible account to ensure it's available when needed.

Day 273

Create the life you want.

Life doesn't just unfold according to your wishes; it requires effort and intention. Suppose you don't actively shape your future by setting goals, making plans, and taking meaningful actions. In that case, you might find yourself stuck in situations or circumstances that you find unfulfilling or stressful. Taking charge of your life means making choices that align with your values and aspirations, even if challenging. By doing the work now, you're investing in a future that reflects your desires and dreams. On the other hand, neglecting to take control can lead to a life where you're constantly managing problems, regrets, or someone else's dreams.

Day 274

Be open to moving for the right job.

Securing your dream role or advancing your career sometimes requires relocating to a new city or state. While moving can be a significant change, it can also open doors to exciting opportunities and experiences. Consider the potential benefits, such as career growth, better salary, or a vibrant job market in your new location. Weigh these advantages against the challenges of relocating, like adjusting to a new environment or being away from family and friends. If the job aligns with your career goals and offers substantial benefits, the move could be a worthwhile investment in your future. Approach the relocation with a positive mindset and take the opportunity to explore and enjoy a new place.

Day 275

You think college is tough? Wait until you get a boss.

While teachers set ambitious standards and challenge you to perform academically, a boss will hold you accountable for your work, professionalism, and results. Your boss's feedback might be more direct and focused on achieving business objectives, which can be a big shift from the structured environment of school. Embrace this challenge as an opportunity to develop resilience and adapt your skills. Approach feedback with a positive attitude and use it to improve and grow. The workplace demands technical skills, strong problem-solving abilities, effective communication, and teamwork.

Day 276

Most things are more rewarding when you break a sweat.

Hard work and effort often lead to a deeper sense of accomplishment and satisfaction. When you invest time and energy into something, you develop skills, build resilience, and gain valuable experience along the way. The sense of pride and fulfillment that comes from achieving something through hard work is often more profound than if handed to you effortlessly. Embrace the challenges and put in the effort, knowing that the rewards will be much sweeter. The journey and the struggles you overcome make the successes genuinely gratifying. So, roll up your sleeves, get involved, and give it your all—your dedication will make the results even more rewarding.

Day 277

Thank the people who made a difference in your life.

It may sound old school, but handwritten notes can make a powerful impression and set you apart. In a world dominated by digital communication, writing a personal, handwritten note shows genuine appreciation and thoughtfulness. It's a simple yet meaningful gesture that can leave a lasting impact on those who have supported, guided, or inspired you. This small act of kindness strengthens your relationships, makes you memorable, and demonstrates your character. By acknowledging the contributions of others, you build positive connections and create a ripple effect of goodwill and appreciation. Your gratitude will be remembered.

Day 278

What you say and do might be forgotten, but the way you make others feel will leave a lasting impression.

While your words and actions matter now, the lasting impact comes from how you treat people. If you take the time to make someone feel valued, heard, or supported, that's what they'll carry with them long after the conversation ends. This goes both ways—negative interactions will also linger if you make someone feel disrespected or dismissed. Pay attention to how your actions and words make others feel because building positive relationships is key to personal and professional success. Treat people with empathy and sincerity, and you'll create meaningful connections and develop a reputation as someone who genuinely cares.

Day 279

Sometimes, you just have to throw out the plan.

Sure, having goals and direction is important, but don't get so locked into a plan that you miss out on unexpected chances. Sometimes, the best things happen when you veer off course, take a risk, or say "Yes" to an opportunity that wasn't part of the original agenda. Whether it's a new job, an inspiring class, or an unexpected friendship, these moments can shape your future in ways you never imagined. Luck often comes from being open, adaptable, and willing to act when opportunities arise. Plans are helpful guides, but don't be afraid to adjust, explore, and create your path.

Day 280

Massive screw-ups can bring amazing opportunities.

Mistakes happen, especially in college and early adulthood, and can feel like the end of the world. But here's the thing: those mess-ups often teach you the lessons you need to grow and find your path. Maybe you bombed an interview or completely fumbled a project. In the moment, it's tough, but those setbacks can open doors you never expected. That failed attempt might push you to explore new interests, meet different people, or develop skills you didn't know you had. The key is not to dwell on the mistake but to learn from it and pivot. Sometimes, the best opportunities come from being forced to take a different direction. So, when you screw up—and you will—take a breath, figure out what you can learn, and keep moving forward.

Day 281

Don't be afraid of growing slowly; be afraid of standing still.

Real growth, academic, personal, or professional, often comes in small, steady steps. It's easy to feel frustrated when you're not moving as fast as you'd like or when it seems like others are speeding ahead, but the key is to keep moving forward, even if it's at your own pace. What matters is that you're progressing, learning, and evolving. Standing still, however, is where the real danger lies. You miss out on growth opportunities when you stop challenging yourself or avoid taking risks because of fear or uncertainty. Don't get discouraged by slow progress—every step forward, no matter how small, adds up over time.

Day 282

Wanting to be someone else is a waste of who you are.

It's easy to look at other people and think they have it all together—the perfect career, social life, or confidence. But chasing someone else's life or trying to mimic their path only pulls you further away from your true potential. You were born with your own set of talents, interests, and strengths, and those are what make you unique. Trying to be someone else diminishes what you have to offer the world. Instead of comparing yourself to others, focus on what makes you stand out. Lean into your quirks, passions, and individuality, those are the things that will make your journey fulfilling and help you find success on your own terms. The world doesn't need another version of someone else; it needs the real you.

Day 283

It can be difficult to envision an undefined future.

Life rarely follows a clear-cut plan, and the pressure to define your future can feel overwhelming. But that uncertainty also holds potential. An undefined future means you have the freedom to explore, try new things, and discover passions you didn't even know existed. Instead of stressing over not having a perfect blueprint, embrace the unknown as a place of possibility. You don't need to have all the answers right now. Focus on what excites you in the present, take small steps toward your interests, and remain open to opportunities that come your way. Sometimes, the best path isn't the one you planned but the one you discovered.

Day 284

Decisions are easy when values are clear.

Your values—what you stand for and believe in—act like a compass, guiding you through life's tough decisions. When you're clear about your priorities, you'll naturally lean toward the choices that align with those beliefs. This clarity saves you from second-guessing and makes even the most complicated decisions feel more straightforward. Whether choosing a job, a relationship, or taking the next step in your life, knowing your values ensures that you're making decisions that are true to who you are. It takes the guesswork out of life, allowing you to move forward confidently.

Day 285

Please yourself before you please others.

It's easy to fall into the trap of constantly trying to make everyone around you happy, especially in college, where there's pressure to fit in, impress professors, or meet friends' expectations. But here's the reality—you can't pour from an empty cup. If you spend all your energy trying to satisfy everyone else, you'll feel drained and unfulfilled. Prioritize your well-being, goals, and happiness first. This doesn't mean being selfish; it means setting boundaries, knowing your limits, and ensuring your needs are met before taking on everyone else's problems. When you take care of yourself physically, mentally, and emotionally, you're in a much better position to show up for others in a meaningful way.

Day 286

Listen to your inner self... there is wisdom within.

Deep down, you often know what's right for you, even when the world around you is full of noise and opinions. Trusting your instincts and paying attention to your inner voice can help guide you through tough decisions. While others may have advice, only you truly understand your dreams, values, and what feels right for your path. Your inner self has gathered wisdom from your experiences, challenges, and successes, and tapping into that can provide clarity. Trust that voice—it's there for a reason.

Day 287

Satisfaction lies in doing what others said couldn't be done.

As you prepare to graduate from college and step into the world, you'll encounter plenty of doubts and skepticism from others about your ambitions. Rather than letting these doubts discourage you, use them as motivation to prove yourself. When you take on challenges and push past the limits others set for you, you achieve personal goals and experience the deep satisfaction of proving the naysayers wrong. The path to success often involves breaking barriers and challenging the status quo. So, when faced with doubts or negative opinions, let them drive you to work harder and reach higher.

Day 288

It's better to be hated for what you are than
loved for what you are not.

Trying to meet someone else's expectations or pretending to be something you're not leaves you feeling unfulfilled and disconnected from yourself. Authenticity is powerful. The truth is, it's impossible to please everyone. But when you live genuinely, the people who matter will appreciate you for exactly who you are, not the version of yourself you feel pressured to create. Living authentically allows you to build strong relationships and live a life that aligns with your values and passions. In the long run, you'll feel more satisfied being your true self—even if it ruffles some feathers.

Day 289

What you do when losing track of time is what you should be doing for the rest of your life.

The activities you naturally gravitate toward, even when you're supposed to focus on something else, often reflect your true passions and interests. If you find yourself consistently drawn to specific projects or hobbies during your downtime, it might be a sign that these are areas where you could find great fulfillment and success. Pay attention to what excites you and keeps you engaged, even when distractions are tempting. Embrace these moments of creative flow and curiosity as they may guide you toward a career path that feels both satisfying and authentic.

Day 290

Wherever you go, go with all your heart.

Whether you're starting a new job, pursuing a passion, or simply exploring new interests, pouring your heart into it makes a world of difference. When you approach each situation with enthusiasm and dedication, you maximize your potential and enrich your own experience and the lives of those around you. Being wholehearted means embracing challenges, taking risks, and investing in your endeavors with passion and effort. This approach helps you achieve your goals and ensures you find deeper satisfaction and joy in your work. As you step into new chapters of your academic, personal, or professional life, do so with full commitment and enthusiasm.

Day 291

*If you are brave enough to say "Goodbye," life
will reward you with a new "Hello."*

Letting go of familiar situations, relationships, or even goals that no longer serve you can be incredibly challenging, but it often opens the door to fresh opportunities and new beginnings. Embracing the courage to move on makes space for new experiences and connections that can enrich your life in unexpected ways. Every ending is a prelude to a new chapter filled with potential and promise. By acknowledging that goodbyes can lead to positive transformations, you allow yourself to welcome new opportunities with an open heart and a fresh perspective.

Day 292

*Is what you're doing today getting you closer
to where you want to be tomorrow.*

Getting caught up in immediate tasks or distractions is easy, but regularly assessing your progress can keep you focused and motivated. Are your current activities and choices moving you in the direction of your dreams? If not, it might be time to reassess and adjust your strategies. You can create a more intentional and fulfilling path forward by staying mindful of your goals and ensuring that your daily efforts contribute to your future success. Remember, every step you take—no matter how small—can bring you closer to achieving your ambitions.

Day 293

*Looking back at life, you will be more disappointed
by what you chose not to do.*

As you navigate college and your early career, it's easy to let fear or doubt hold you back from pursuing your dreams or trying new things. However, the missed opportunities and unexplored paths often lead to the greatest regrets later. By daring to step out of your comfort zone and embrace new experiences, you set yourself up for growth, learning, and fulfillment. Whether traveling abroad, starting a passion project, or taking on a challenging job, don't let the fear of failure or the unknown keep you from making the most of your time. Remember, it is not the mistakes or risks that will weigh on you but the chances you didn't take.

Day 294

*If no role models are paving the way for you,
be one yourself.*

As you enter the next phase of your life after college, you might find yourself in environments without clear examples. The lack of established role models doesn't mean you should feel lost or discouraged. Instead, see it as an opportunity to carve your path and become a role model for others. Leading with integrity, pursuing your passions, and overcoming obstacles sets a precedent for those who come after you. Embrace the challenge of being a trailblazer and understand that your actions and achievements will pave the way for others to follow.

Day 295

Time spent doing something you enjoy is never wasted.

In the chaos of college life and the transition into the workforce, it's easy to feel guilty about spending time on hobbies or leisure activities. However, these moments of enjoyment are crucial for your well-being and personal growth. They provide a much-needed break from stress, fuel creativity, and contribute to a balanced life. Engaging in activities you love— reading, hiking, painting, or simply hanging out with friends—allows you to recharge and maintain your mental health. Don't view your downtime as wasted; instead, see it as an investment in your happiness and resilience.

Day 296

The meaning of life is to find your gift; the purpose of life is to give it away.

As you prepare to graduate from college and embark on your career, focus first on identifying what you're truly passionate about and where your strengths lie. Discovering your unique talents and interests is crucial in finding fulfillment and direction. However, the real impact comes when you use those gifts to benefit others. Whether through your career, volunteer work, or personal interactions, sharing your talents and skills can make a significant difference in the lives of those around you. Giving back and using your abilities to help others creates a sense of purpose and builds a legacy beyond personal success.

Day 297

Act on your goals, not your emotions.

In life, you'll encounter moments where feelings of doubt, excitement, or frustration might tempt you to stray from your course. Instead, anchor yourself to your long-term goals. By consistently aligning your actions with your overarching objectives, you ensure that each step you take moves you closer to your aspirations. Remember, emotions are fleeting, but the commitment to your goals provides a steady compass. Focus on your goals and let that vision guide your decisions. This approach will help you maintain your course, overcome obstacles with resilience, and ultimately achieve the success you've set out to reach. Trust in the process and keep your eyes on the prize.

Day 298

Follow your heart, but take your brain with you.

Chasing your dreams is great, but you need to balance that enthusiasm with practical thinking. While your heart will guide you toward what makes you happy, your brain helps you weigh risks, consider consequences, and make wise decisions. As you move forward in life, blending passion with logic ensures you won't get caught up in something that may feel right in the moment, but could hurt you in the long run. The key is to let your heart spark your ambition while your mind keeps you grounded, ensuring you take smart, thoughtful steps.

Day 299

If you focus on what truly interests you, you'll always find satisfaction in pleasing yourself.

You're guaranteed to be happy when you follow your passions and do what excites you. While it's easy to get caught up in trying to meet other people's expectations, living for others can leave you feeling unfulfilled. When you focus on what truly interests you, life becomes more enjoyable, and that satisfaction radiates outward. You can't please everyone, but you can always please yourself by staying true to your interests. And here's the thing: when you're genuinely happy doing what you love, others will notice and respect that authenticity. You'll attract people who appreciate you for who you are, and that's worth more than trying to be everything to everyone.

Day 300

The greatest gift you can give yourself is honesty.

When you're truthful about your feelings, strengths, and flaws, you give yourself the power to make real progress. It's easy to fall into the trap of telling yourself what you want to hear or avoiding brutal truths, but that only holds you back. Honesty helps you see things clearly and allows you to focus on what you need to improve or what truly makes you happy. It also frees you from pretending or living up to unrealistic expectations. When you embrace the truth about who you are, what you want, and where you're headed, you can move forward confidently and authentically.

Day 301

*Failure can be disappointing but not trying
guarantees missed opportunities.*

Fear of failure is real, but not taking a chance is far worse. You can always learn, grow, and try again if you fail. Failure is a part of the process; though it may sting, it's temporary. On the other hand, never trying leaves you wondering what could have been. It creates regret, and that lasts much longer than any temporary disappointment. Taking risks is how you discover what you're capable of, and even when things don't go as planned, the courage to try opens doors to new opportunities. Trying is how you move forward; without that step, you'll never know what you can achieve.

Day 302

Today, be the badass you were too lazy to be yesterday.

Yesterday's excuses, distractions, or moments of procrastination are in the past. You have the opportunity today to bring the energy, determination, and grit you know you can. It's easy to settle for the bare minimum, but deep down, you know you can do more and be more. So, why not decide to go all in today? Take that step toward your goals, push yourself a little more, and embrace the effort it takes to be truly exceptional. Being a 'badass' isn't about perfection but showing up with focus and determination, even when it's hard. Leave yesterday's laziness behind and make today count.

Day 303

There's always a risk of failure, even in things you enjoy.

Playing it safe doesn't guarantee success; sometimes, even the most secure choices can lead to disappointment. If failure is a possibility no matter what, why not aim for something that genuinely excites you? When you go after what you love, you're not just chasing a goal but pursuing passion, meaning, and fulfillment. The risks might seem more significant, but so are the rewards. Imagine pouring your energy into something you care about. Even if things don't turn out as planned, you'll still be proud of taking that leap. And if it works out? You'll have built a life doing what brings you joy. Don't settle for what's "safe" because it seems like the responsible choice. Go for what sets your soul on fire, you'll never regret taking that chance.

Day 304

You create opportunities by performing, not complaining.

You create momentum when you show up, do the work, and focus on results. Opportunities come to those who prove themselves capable, reliable, and focused on solutions. Complaining may feel good in the moment, but it doesn't move you forward. It's your performance, your effort, and your willingness to solve problems that opens doors. People notice those who step up when challenges arise and look for ways to improve rather than find excuses. Every time you act, you build your reputation as someone who delivers, and that's where opportunities are born.

Day 305

Set a big goal you can't achieve until you grow into someone who can.

A goal that feels just out of reach isn't meant to discourage you, it's meant to inspire growth. When you aim high, you're not just working toward an outcome but also working on becoming the person who can handle the challenges of achieving it. Big goals require persistence, learning, and sometimes even failure. But with each step, you gain the skills, confidence, and mindset needed to succeed. It's not just about reaching the finish line; it's about who you become along the way. So, dream big, because growing into that goal will be one of the most rewarding parts of your life. You'll look back and realize that the person who started wouldn't have been ready for the success you're building toward—but the person you've grown into will be.

Day 306

You are defined by the choices you make.

Big or small choices contribute to your character, path, and future. It's important to remember that each choice reflects your values, goals, and vision for your life. Whether you're deciding on your career, relationships, or daily habits, make choices that align with who you want to be and where you want to go. Wisely chosen actions build a foundation for success and fulfillment, while poor choices can lead to setbacks and regret. Consider your options, weigh the potential outcomes, and choose with intention

Day 307

A path without obstacles likely doesn't lead to anything meaningful.

If everything was smooth and easy, it might mean you're following a well-used path, offering little opportunity for growth or discovery. The most rewarding journeys usually involve overcoming difficulties, learning from setbacks, and pushing through adversity. These challenges test your resolve and shape your character and skills. Embrace obstacles as a natural part of the journey because they often lead to the most valuable experiences and achievements. A path without hurdles might be comfortable, but the tough roads lead to significant accomplishments and personal growth.

Day 308

Don't let short-term emotions affect long-term goals.

Emotions are fleeting and can cloud your judgment, leading you to make decisions based on temporary feelings rather than your broader objectives. Instead, anchor your actions in your long-term vision and values. When faced with emotional ups and downs, remind yourself of the bigger picture and the reasons behind your goals. This perspective helps you stay on track, make thoughtful decisions, and maintain consistency in your efforts. Lasting success often requires discipline and resilience, so let your long-term vision guide you rather than allowing short-term emotions derail your progress.

Day 309

The regret of not following your heart lingers for a lifetime.

Ignoring what truly matters to you in favor of playing it safe or meeting others' expectations can lead to deep regret. When you let fear or conformity dictate your choices, you risk living a life that doesn't fulfill you. Following your heart involves taking risks, pursuing passions, and making decisions that align with your deepest desires. While it might be challenging or uncertain, the fulfillment that comes from living authentically is worth it. Imagine looking back on your life with no regrets because you dared to follow what you truly wanted.

Day 310

When in doubt, a business major.

If you're unsure about your major, consider this: a business degree is one of the most versatile options out there. No matter where life takes you, understanding finance, marketing, management, and economics will always be beneficial. A business degree teaches you how to think strategically, solve problems, and communicate effectively—skills that employers love and that can help you in any industry. You don't have to commit to being a CEO, but having a business background gives you options. And in a world where flexibility is key, that's a major advantage. So, if you're stuck, a business degree might just be the safest bet with the biggest payoff.

Finding Your Passion and Purpose

Figuring out your purpose can feel overwhelming, but it doesn't have to be. This exercise will help you explore your interests, strengths, and experiences so you can start building a path that excites and fulfills you.

- **Explore Your Interests:** Take a variety of classes, join clubs, and meet different people. Pay attention to what excites you—your purpose often starts with curiosity.

- **Identify Your Strengths:** What do people naturally turn to you for? What subjects or activities come easily to you? Your skills can guide you toward meaningful work.

- **Try, Fail, and Learn:** Say yes to side projects, internships, and leadership roles. Some experiences will click, others won't—that's how you refine what matters to you.

- **Connect with Like-Minded People:** Seek mentors, network with professionals, and engage with communities that share your interests. Purpose grows in conversations and shared experiences.

- **Align Passion with Impact:** Ask yourself: "How can I use my talents to contribute?" Purpose isn't just about what you love to do—it's about how it benefits others, too.

- **Stay Open to Change:** Your purpose isn't set in stone. As you grow, so will your direction. Keep learning, adapting, and chasing what truly fulfills you.

Chapter 6
Life Beyond College: Preparing for the Real World

Day 311

Some of the best opportunities come from networking.

Networking isn't just for job hunting, it's a key part of building a successful career, and you should start while you're still in college. Reach out to professors, attend industry events, and connect with guest speakers. Join student organizations related to your field and take part in internships or volunteer opportunities where you can meet professionals. Each person you meet has their own network, and by making a positive impression, you open doors to new opportunities and valuable advice. Remember, networking is a two-way street: offer both help and support to others. Building genuine relationships based on mutual respect and shared interests will pay off in the long run. Start now, and by the time you graduate, you'll have a solid network that can assist you in landing your first job and advancing your career.

Day 312

Today is a great day to be proud of how far you've come.

Take a moment to reflect on your journey, how you've tackled challenges, learned new skills, and grown into the person you are now. Graduating college is an achievement, and it's important to recognize the hard work, dedication, and perseverance that got you there. Celebrate your successes and acknowledge the obstacles you've overcome throughout your college experience. Embrace this sense of pride and use it as motivation. Give yourself credit for every step you've taken and every goal you've achieved. Being proud of your progress fuels your confidence and sets the stage for continued success.

Day 313

Pay no more than 30% of your income on rent.

When you start budgeting for your own place, calculate your monthly income and stick to this 30% cap to keep your finances in check. This approach helps prevent financial stress and allows you to allocate funds toward building an emergency fund, paying for school supplies, and enjoying a balanced lifestyle. Finding an affordable place might take some time, but staying within this limit is worth the effort.

Tip: If you need a roommate to afford post-college housing, approach it as a professional agreement, not another frat house.

Day 314

If you mess up, it's not your parents' fault.

Mistakes are a natural part of life, and everyone makes them—what matters most is how you handle them. Blaming others, including your parents, can prevent you from learning and growing. Instead, focus on what you can do to fix the situation and learn from it. Your parents have supported and guided you, but ultimately, you take charge of your choices. Taking ownership of your actions helps you become more resilient and self-reliant. It's an important step toward independence and personal growth. Maturity means understanding that while your parents have been there for you, your path is yours to navigate.

Day 315

Living in an expensive city can rob the joy of a good job.

High rent, steep prices for everyday items, and the cost of dining out or entertainment can quickly add up, leaving you with little to enjoy the fruits of your hard work. When the cost of living consumes a large portion of your salary, it can lead to stress and financial strain, overshadowing the satisfaction of a successful career. To avoid this, consider your budget carefully before committing to a city with a high cost of living. Explore areas where the expenses are more manageable, and you can still find opportunities that align with your career goals. Remember, a job should enhance your life, not dominate it with financial worries.

Day 316

Possessions should be few and low maintenance.

Simplifying your belongings makes moving easier, reduces stress, and frees up time for things that truly matter. Choose items that require minimal care and don't take up too much space. This approach will help you avoid clutter and focus on experiences rather than things. When selecting possessions, consider how each item will fit into your lifestyle and whether it adds value or takes up space. By keeping your possessions streamlined, you can maintain a sense of order and control, contributing to a more balanced and fulfilling life. Embrace the freedom of having fewer things to manage and enjoy the flexibility of a more simplified lifestyle.

Day 317

Live like a college student after graduation!

Even after graduation, live like a college student and watch your savings grow. Embrace a frugal lifestyle by sticking to a tight budget, avoiding unnecessary splurges, and keeping your expenses low. Opt for simple meals, skip expensive coffee runs, and choose budget-friendly entertainment. This doesn't mean you can't enjoy yourself, but it's about prioritizing financial stability over instant gratification. By saving and investing a significant portion of your income now, you'll build a strong financial foundation for your future, whether buying a home, starting a business, or just having a safety net.

Day 318

*When starting out, it's ok to set your sights
a tad below your dream job.*

While having big dreams and ambitious goals is great, remember that landing a job that matches your passion and vision might take time. Starting with a role that offers solid experience, a good work environment, and growth opportunities can be a smart move. Focus on finding a position where you can learn, develop new skills, and build a professional network. Over time, as you gain experience and clarity about your true passions, you can steer your career toward more exciting opportunities. Be open to various roles and experiences to lay a solid foundation for future success.

Day 319

It may take many baby steps to find your dream job.

Don't be discouraged if you don't land your ideal position immediately. Start by taking small actions: refine your resume, network with professionals, apply for internships, or take on part-time work related to your field. Each step, no matter how minor it seems, builds experience and brings you closer to your goal. Stay persistent and keep pushing forward, even if progress feels slow. Use every opportunity to learn, grow, and make connections. Over time, these efforts will accumulate, guiding you closer to that dream job. Keep stepping, stay motivated, and trust that every little action contributes to your career path.

Day 320

Even the mightiest oak tree began as a tiny nut.

Even if they don't seem impressive, early jobs lay the foundation for your future success. They offer valuable experiences, skills, and connections you'll build upon as you progress. Every bit of effort you put in now, no matter how small, contributes to your long-term career and personal development. Be patient and persistent, like that little nut growing into a mighty oak. Your career will take time to develop, but every experience helps shape your path and prepares you for more significant opportunities. Keep a positive attitude and focus on the skills and knowledge you're gaining. Even the most successful people started with humble beginnings.

Day 321

Customize your resume for each job opportunity.

A one-size-fits-all resume won't make you stand out. Tailor your resume to match the specific skills, experiences, and qualifications each job requires. Start by carefully reading the job description and highlighting the key skills and experiences the employer is looking for. Then, adjust your resume to emphasize how your background aligns with those requirements. Include relevant achievements and use keywords from the job posting to ensure your resume is noticed by both automated systems and hiring managers. Customizing your resume shows that you're genuinely interested in the position and have tried to match your qualifications with the job.

Day 322

Pay off student loans as soon as possible.

Starting early to pay off your student loans can make a huge difference to the total amount you'll pay. The sooner you begin, the less interest you'll accumulate, and the faster you'll free yourself from debt. Consider making extra payments whenever you can, even if they're small. Staying on top of your payments helps maintain a good credit score.

Tip: Avoid sticking to just minimal payments, or you could find yourself still paying off student loans when it's time to retire.

Day 323

Never walk out on a job; be professional and give notice.

Quitting a job abruptly can harm your reputation and leave a negative impression on future employers. Instead, give your employer a proper notice period, typically two weeks, for a smooth transition. This approach respects the company and helps maintain positive relationships with colleagues and supervisors. A well-handled departure also ensures that you leave on good terms, which could be beneficial if you need references or want to return to the company in the future. Craft a thoughtful resignation letter and offer to help train your replacement if possible. By leaving professionally, you demonstrate maturity and responsibility, qualities that are valued in any career. How you exit a job can be just as important as how you performed while you were there.

Day 324

Never cash out a retirement account early.

Cashing out a retirement account early might seem tempting, but that often means facing hefty penalties and paying income tax on the withdrawn amount. The money you withdraw won't have the chance to accumulate interest or grow through investments, which can significantly reduce your retirement nest egg. Instead, consider exploring other financial options or budgeting strategies to manage your current needs. Keeping your retirement account intact ensures you build a solid financial foundation for your future.

Day 325

Use whatever resources the college has to prepare yourself for life after school.

Colleges provide a wealth of tools to help you succeed beyond the campus. Take advantage of career services for resume building, job search strategies, and interview preparation. Many schools offer networking events, internships, and job fairs that connect you with potential employers and industry professionals. Explore academic advising to ensure you're on track with your course load and graduation requirements. Use the library and online databases for research and skill development. Attending workshops and seminars on financial literacy, personal development, and job market trends. Connect with alumni who can offer valuable insights and mentorship.

Day 326

"Try not to become a man of success, but rather a man of value." — Albert Einstein

---

Success often follows when you genuinely contribute to others' lives and stand by your principles. Build relationships based on respect and kindness and strive to improve the world around you. Seek to add value through your work by solving problems and helping others. Understand that true fulfillment comes from making a difference, not merely from accolades or financial rewards. Your reputation and impact will grow naturally from your commitment to doing good work and treating others well.

Day 327

This is the easiest time to start your own business because you will likely have fewer obligations.

Seize the opportunity to start your own business while it's easier. You may have fewer responsibilities, which means you can take risks and pursue your entrepreneurial dreams. Having fewer obligations makes this the perfect time to experiment, learn, and grow. You can focus on your passion, invest time and energy into building something from scratch, and adapt quickly without the constraints that come with other commitments. Taking this step now might not guarantee immediate success, but it will provide invaluable experience and set the stage for future growth.

Day 328

Think hard before welcoming children or pets into your life.

Both children and pets come with significant commitments beyond providing food and shelter. They both need your time, attention, emotional and financial investment. They can add joy to your life but require consistent care and support. Managing their needs can be challenging, especially if you're starting your career and juggling new responsibilities. Before making this decision, consider your current and future obligations. Are you ready to handle the added responsibilities? Reflect on your lifestyle and career goals, than ask if now's the right time.

Day 329

Think carefully about whether buying or renting suits your finances, lifestyle, and future goals.

Owning a home might sound like the smart, "grown-up" thing, but it's not always the best choice out of college. Buying a home ties you down to one location, and there are a lot of extra costs. If your career might take you to different cities or you're not sure where you want to settle, renting gives you flexibility without the extra headaches. On the other hand, buying could be a good investment if you know where you want to live long-term and have a steady income. Renting can help you build savings and give you more financial breathing room, while owning builds equity over time. Weigh the pros and cons, and make sure your choice aligns with your lifestyle and future plans.

Day 330

There's more to a great job offer than a killer salary.

Instead of focusing solely on the salary, look for employers that offer growth potential. Seek out companies where you can learn, develop your skills, and advance over time. A job with room for growth can lead to better opportunities and higher pay in the future. Consider factors like professional development programs, mentorship, and the company's track record for promotion from within. These aspects can be more valuable in the long run than an immediate high salary.

Day 331

Just because you have a degree, don't get cocky.

A diploma shows you've worked hard and learned much, but it's not a golden ticket to instant success. In the real world, people care more about what you can do than the piece of paper you earned. Employers want to see your work ethic, problem-solving skills, and how well you handle challenges. The degree opens doors, but it's up to you to walk through them by staying humble, continuing to learn, and proving yourself. Be open to advice, mentorship, and feedback because there's always something new to learn. Remember, no one likes arrogance — confidence is good, but cockiness can push people away. Real growth comes from understanding that a degree is just the beginning. Stay grounded, curious, and be ready to prove that you're more than just what's written on your resume.

Day 332

Never accept a job simply because it's higher pay.

When you graduate, jumping at the job that offers the highest paycheck is tempting. But don't let the dollar signs blind you. A bigger salary doesn't always mean a better life. You might find yourself in a toxic work environment, doing work that drains your energy, or working crazy hours that leave you with little time to enjoy life. Money can only do so much to make you happy if you're stuck in a job that makes you miserable. Instead, look for a job that challenges you, helps you grow, and aligns with your passions and values. A job that fits you well can lead to more opportunities and, eventually, the higher salary you want — but with balance and fulfillment. Think long-term and remember that your happiness and well-being are worth more than a big paycheck.

Day 333

Dress better than the dress code.

Dressing better than expected conveys that you're ready for more significant opportunities, even if you're just starting out in your career. People notice when you put in extra effort, and how you present yourself plays a big part. Dressing well doesn't mean buying expensive clothes, but choosing polished, professional, and appropriate outfits for your workplace. You'll stand out in a good way, and it can even boost your confidence. Plus, you never know who you'll run into — whether it's a potential mentor, a future boss, or a high-profile client.

Day 334

Stop being afraid of what could go wrong.

Sure, things might not always go perfectly, that's life, but if you let fear run the show, you'll miss out on some amazing opportunities. Every new challenge or decision has the potential for success, growth, and excitement. Taking risks, whether in your career, relationships, or personal goals, can lead to some of the best moments in life. You'll learn something valuable even if things don't go as planned. Being positive doesn't mean ignoring challenges, rather it's about believing in your ability to handle them. Don't let fear steal your future.

Day 335

There is a huge difference between getting
an education and being educated.

Getting an education means you've completed classes, earned a degree, and followed the rules to graduate. But being educated goes deeper. Just because you have a diploma doesn't mean you know everything. Life will keep teaching you lessons long after you leave the classroom, and real wisdom comes from being curious, asking questions, and challenging yourself. Being educated means you're not afraid to admit when you don't know something and are willing to grow from good and bad experiences. It's about understanding different perspectives, seeking out new ideas, and using what you know to solve problems and make a positive impact.

Day 336

Consider teaching your native language abroad.

Teaching your native language abroad allows you to experience life in another country, meet new people, and fully immerse yourself in a different culture. Plus, it's a great way to break away from the traditional 9-to-5 routine and do something adventurous before you settle into a long-term career. Employers love seeing diverse experiences on a resume, and teaching abroad shows that you're adaptable, independent, and willing to step out of your comfort zone. You'll also gain valuable communication, leadership, and problem-solving skills to stand out in future job interviews. On top of that, you'll have the chance to travel, explore new places, and create memories that will last a lifetime.

Tip: Check for opportunities with Peace Corps or WorldTeach; or contact International TEFL Academy or TEFL.org.

Day 337

Buy the cheapest house in the nicest neighborhood.

When you're ready to buy a house, remember that the location is something you can't change, and it plays a massive role in your quality of life and the future value of your property. By choosing a home in a desirable area, you're investing in a location that's likely to become more valuable over time, which can be a smart financial move.

Day 338

Max out retirement contributions while expenses are low.

Maxing out your retirement account contributions while your expenses are still low is one of the smartest financial moves you can make right out of college. By contributing the maximum amount to your retirement accounts now, like a 401(k) or IRA, you're giving your money more time to grow through compound interest. Even small contributions can snowball into something significant over time. Plus, many employers offer matching contributions to your 401(k), so not taking advantage of that is like leaving free money on the table. The earlier you start, the more your investments will grow, and the less you'll have to worry about playing catch-up later.

Day 339

Stuff won't make you happy.

It's easy to think that the latest gadgets, fashionable clothes, or a big house will make you feel fulfilled, but true happiness comes from much more than material things. The joy you get from new possessions is often short-lived, and once the excitement wears off, you're left searching for the next thing to fill that gap. Instead of focusing on what you can buy, invest in experiences and relationships that bring you genuine joy. Spend time with friends and family, travel to new places, and pursue hobbies and passions that make you feel alive. Building meaningful connections and creating lasting memories will offer more profound satisfaction than any new purchase.

Day 340

If you spend your life chasing some hard-to-obtain thing, you will likely be disappointed once you finally get it.

The problem with fixating on one goal is that it's easy to lose sight of everything else that matters along the way. You start to believe that once you reach that goal, everything will magically fall into place, and you'll be happy. But the truth is, happiness doesn't come from achieving just one thing — it comes from the journey, the experiences, and the people you meet along the way. When you finally get what you've been chasing, it might not feel as satisfying as you thought because you've built it up in your mind for so long. Instead of putting all your energy into one elusive goal, focus on enjoying life as it happens. Set goals, work hard, but don't let the pursuit consume you.

Day 341

Volunteer for something you believe in.

Whether it's helping at a local shelter, working with environmental groups, or supporting education initiatives, volunteering allows you to make a meaningful impact while also discovering more about yourself and your values. It's a great way to meet people who share your interests, build connections, and gain new skills to enhance your resume. Plus, it can provide a sense of purpose and fulfillment that's hard to find elsewhere. Don't just look at volunteer opportunities as something to add to your list; choose something that excites you and aligns with your personal beliefs.

Day 342

Travel as much as possible.

Traveling while you're young and free allows you to immerse yourself in different cultures, meet new people, and create unforgettable experiences. It's an opportunity to broaden your horizons and gain perspectives that can shape your personal and professional life. Plus, adapting and taking risks is easier when you don't have a lot tying you down. Whether backpacking through Europe, volunteering abroad, or simply exploring nearby cities, each trip will teach you something new and offer valuable lessons. You'll build memories, learn about yourself, and discover what truly excites you. The experiences you gather now will enrich your life and give you stories to tell for years to come.

Day 343

Do what makes you happy.

While a high salary might seem like the goal, true fulfillment often comes from pursuing work that aligns with your passions and values. When you choose a career or job that genuinely excites and motivates you, you're more likely to enjoy your work, stay engaged, and find a sense of purpose. Happiness and job satisfaction can significantly impact your well-being and quality of life. Consider what activities and roles bring you joy, challenge you, and allow you to grow. Pursue opportunities that resonate with your interests and strengths, even if they don't offer the highest paycheck.

Day 344

There are no shortcuts to wealth.

It's tempting to look for quick ways to get rich, whether through risky investments or flashy schemes, but true financial success comes from hard work, patience, and thoughtful planning. Wealth isn't built overnight; it takes time to grow and requires consistent effort. Focus on setting clear goals, creating a solid financial plan, and sticking to it. Save regularly, invest wisely, and avoid getting caught up in get-rich-quick schemes that promise fast results but often lead to disappointment. Building wealth involves understanding how to manage your money, live within your means, and making informed decisions. The most successful people stay disciplined, keep learning about personal finance, and progress steadily over time. Building wealth is a marathon, not a sprint. Embrace the process and be patient with your progress.

Day 345

Research a prospective employer to be sure it's a good fit.

Before committing to a job, take the time to thoroughly investigate the company to ensure it aligns with your values, career goals, and work style. Look into the company's culture, mission, and work environment by reading reviews, talking to current or former employees, and exploring their website and social media presence. Assess whether their values and goals resonate with you and whether their work culture suits your preferences. A job is more than just a paycheck; it's an integral part of your professional life.

Day 346

The most qualified person doesn't always get the job.

Employers often look for someone with the right skills who fits well with the team and shows genuine enthusiasm and commitment. They want to see that you're passionate about the role, willing to learn, and ready to contribute positively to the workplace culture. Being personable, showing a strong work ethic, and demonstrating that you care about the company's mission can make a big difference. Your attitude, energy, and willingness to go the extra mile can set you apart from other candidates who might have more experience but less drive. Your enthusiasm can often be as important as your qualifications and help you stand out.

Day 347

If it sounds too good to be true, it probably is.

Scams and shady deals often promise huge rewards with little effort or risk, but they usually become more trouble than they are worth. Use your critical thinking skills, whether it's an investment that promises sky-high returns with no risk, a job offer that sounds too easy, or an unbelievably cheap sale. Research the offer, ask questions, and consult with someone you trust before diving in. If it seems too good to be true, it's often designed to lure you in with enticing promises and then hit you with hidden costs or downsides. Protect yourself by being skeptical of anything that sounds overly optimistic. Stay alert, trust your instincts, and don't rush into anything just because it sounds perfect at first glance.

Day 348

Get in the habit of living within a budget.

It's easy to get caught up in spending when you start earning money, but without a budget, you might find yourself overspending and facing financial stress. Start by tracking your income and expenses to know exactly where your money goes. Set clear limits for different categories like housing, groceries, entertainment, and savings. Living within a budget teaches discipline and control, which are crucial for managing money effectively. Start small if needed and adjust as your financial situation changes, but make budgeting a regular part of your life.

Day 349

Don't assume you'll find your dream job right away.

Many people start with positions that offer valuable experience, even if they aren't perfect or aligned with their ultimate career goals. These roles can help you build skills, gain industry knowledge, and make connections that will benefit you later. It's important to stay open-minded and patient as you navigate the job market. Use this time to explore different fields, understand what you enjoy, and refine your career goals. Your dream job might take a few years to find, and that's okay. Focus on learning and growing in each role you take on, and don't be discouraged if things don't immediately fall into place. Keep a positive attitude, be persistent, and remember that career paths are rarely linear.

Day 350

Soft skills can make or break your career.

Soft skills like teamwork, leadership, problem-solving, and emotional intelligence are just as necessary as technical abilities. They help you build strong relationships with colleagues, navigate office politics, and gracefully handle stressful situations. Employers value team players who collaborate well, adapt to change, and contribute positively to the work environment. Developing these skills can set you apart from others with similar technical expertise but lack the interpersonal qualities that make them effective in a team setting. Invest time improving your soft skills by seeking feedback, practicing communication, and taking on leadership roles.

Day 351

This is the beginning of anything you want.

As you graduate college, remember that you are at the starting point of countless possibilities. The future is wide open, and you have the power to shape it according to your dreams and aspirations. This moment is your opportunity to define what you want to achieve and take the first steps toward making it happen. Whether aiming for a specific career, pursuing further education, or exploring new passions, now is the time to set your goals and act. Embrace the excitement and potential of this fresh start and approach each new challenge with enthusiasm and determination.

Day 352

When you screw up (and you will), own up!

Mistakes are a natural part of life and learning, especially as you start your career and navigate new responsibilities. The key is to take responsibility for your actions instead of making excuses or shifting blame. Owning up to your errors shows maturity, integrity, and a willingness to learn from your experiences. When you admit your mistakes, you gain respect from others and demonstrate that you are accountable and trustworthy. It also allows you to address the issue directly, fix it if possible, and prevent similar problems in the future. Everyone makes mistakes, but how you handle them can set you apart. Apologize, if necessary, take corrective action, and use the experience as a steppingstone for personal and professional growth.

Here is a fess-up formula for when you make a mistake:

- **Acknowledge the mistake clearly and quickly:** Be direct and say, "I messed up, and I take full responsibility."

- **Make it right (if possible):** If there is a way to fix the issue, take action. Put in the effort to apologize, correct the error, and determine how to make it so the mistake will not happen again.

- **Learn from the mistake and move on:** Take time to reflect on what went wrong, adjust your approach and use it as a lesson for the future.

Day 353

If you don't find a job quickly, do something meaningful.

Instead of waiting idly, use this time to stay active and build your skills. Volunteering can help you gain experience, meet new people, and positively impact your community. Traveling can broaden your horizons, provide new perspectives, and offer unique networking opportunities. Taking on temporary or part-time work can help you stay financially afloat while searching for your ideal job and add valuable experience to your resume. The experiences you gain during this period can help you discover new interests, develop new skills, and make you a more well-rounded candidate when you find that perfect job.

Day 354

Graduating college is not the end of learning.

As you step out of the classroom and into the real world, you'll find that education continues in many forms. The knowledge and skills you've gained in college lay the foundation, but the world is constantly changing, and there's so much more to discover. Whether it's through on-the-job experiences, professional development courses, or simply exploring new interests, the learning never stops. Your career, hobbies, and personal life will offer opportunities to expand your knowledge and skills. Stay curious and open-minded and seek out opportunities to learn from every experience. Just because you've earned a diploma doesn't mean you've reached the finish line.

Day 355

Throughout life you will reinvent yourself many times over.

The job market and industries constantly evolve, and staying relevant means adapting to new trends, technologies, and demands. As you advance in your career, you'll likely encounter shifts in your role, industry changes, or even new career paths. Embrace these opportunities to reinvent as a chance to grow and stay engaged. Being flexible and open to change will help you remain competitive. Reinvention doesn't mean starting from scratch; it's about building on your strengths and experiences while adapting to new challenges.

Day 356

Spend your twenties learning a lucrative skill
very well, then milk it for all it's worth.

While dabbling in many fields is tempting, honing one skill to an expert level can lead to higher demand and better pay. Choose a skill that aligns with your interests and has strong earning potential. Invest time and effort into becoming highly proficient, and you'll find that this expertise opens doors to advanced roles, higher salaries, and greater career satisfaction. Once you've achieved a high skill level, leverage it to maximize your career opportunities. This could mean negotiating higher pay, seeking promotions, or exploring niche markets where your expertise is highly valued.

Day 357

Your degree doesn't mean you can run the company.

Earning a degree shows you have the perseverance to complete a challenging academic program, but it's only one part of what it takes to succeed in a professional environment. While your degree is an asset and a testament to your hard work, continuing learning and gaining hands-on experience is essential. Seek internships, lower-level positions, or mentorship opportunities to build the skills and knowledge needed for more significant roles. Approach each opportunity as a chance to grow and develop the competencies necessary for leadership. Professional success comes from education, experience, and the ability to adapt and lead.

Day 358

Greatness is starting something that lives on after you.

True greatness isn't just about personal achievements or accolades; it's about creating something meaningful that continues to leave an impact long after you're gone. This could be a project, a business, a piece of art, or even a legacy of positive change. Focus on projects or goals that align with your passions and values and consider how they can benefit others or inspire future generations. Think about how to make a difference and create something that resonates beyond your lifetime; you achieve personal fulfillment and significantly contribute to your field or community. Remember, the most impactful legacies often continue to grow, evolve, and inspire even after you've moved on.

Day 359

Volunteer for crappy jobs and do them cheerfully.

Instead of avoiding crappy tasks or grumbling, take the initiative and approach these tasks with a positive attitude. Doing the less appealing jobs enthusiastically shows you're a team player willing to contribute wherever needed. It also gives you a chance to demonstrate your work ethic and reliability. By tackling these jobs cheerfully, you make a strong impression and often find that your efforts lead to more interesting and challenging opportunities. Your willingness to take on the tough stuff will set you apart and help you build a solid reputation.

Day 360

Knowing your professors can pay off.

Building strong relationships with your professors while still in college can be incredibly beneficial for your future. Professors who know you well are more likely to write detailed and personalized recommendations that highlight your strengths and accomplishments. Take the time to engage with your professors, participate actively in their classes, and seek their guidance on academic projects. Show genuine interest in their work and build a rapport with them. This way, when requesting a recommendation letter, they'll be familiar with your abilities and achievements, making their endorsements more impactful. Additionally, strong connections with professors can lead to valuable mentorship and advice as you navigate your career path.

Day 361

Get a classic suit or dress for interviews.

Yes, even in today's environment of casual workplace attire, having a timeless, professional outfit can make a big difference. A classic suit or dress conveys confidence, professionalism, and a serious attitude toward the opportunity. If the company has a relaxed culture, it is still important to dress appropriately. Opt for neutral colors like black, navy, or gray, which are versatile and always in style. Make sure your outfit is well-fitted and comfortable, which will help you feel more confident and focused during the interview. First impressions matter and dressing appropriately for the occasion shows respect for the interviewer and the company.

Day 362

Be ready for a lot of change in the next few years.

As you transition from college to the real world, you'll encounter numerous changes in your personal and professional life. These changes might include moving to a new city, starting a new job, or navigating new responsibilities. Embrace this period of transformation with an open mind and a positive attitude. Adaptability and resilience will be your best allies as you face these new challenges and opportunities. Change can be exciting, but it can also be daunting, so stay flexible and proactive. Look at each change as an opportunity for growth and learning. Keep your goals and values focused and be prepared to adjust your plans as needed.

Day 363

Avoid upgrading everything just because you graduated.

It's tempting to make sweeping changes or splurge on new items now that you're entering the workforce, but it's important to be thoughtful about your decisions. Financial responsibility starts with managing your expenses wisely, so resist the urge to buy a new car or upgrade your apartment to mark this new chapter. Instead, focus on building a solid foundation for your future by budgeting and saving for long-term goals. Prioritize needs over wants and make upgrades gradually as your financial situation allows. The value of your achievements isn't in the material upgrades you make but, in the experiences and accomplishments you build over time.

Day 364

Apply for interesting jobs, even if outside of your degree.

Explore roles that align with your interests, skills, and passions, even if they don't directly relate to your degree. Diverse experiences can broaden your skill set and open doors to new industries and opportunities. Sometimes, the most rewarding careers come from unexpected places. Don't be afraid to step outside your comfort zone and pursue positions that intrigue you or align with your personal goals. By applying for jobs that spark your curiosity, you increase your chances of finding a role you enjoy and demonstrate adaptability and a willingness to learn.

Day 365

Leave room for magic.

As you step into college and beyond, remember this: prepare as much as possible, but don't cling too tightly to the plan. Overprepare, learn, and have a clear sense of direction, but when the moment comes, take action and trust yourself to adapt. Life rarely unfolds exactly as we expect, and that's where the magic happens. You often find the most growth, joy, and discovery in the quiet spaces, the unexpected opportunities, and the unplanned detours.

Maybe it's a chance encounter that sparks a lifelong friendship, a class you reluctantly take that changes your career path, or a challenge that reveals a strength you didn't know you had. Having a plan gives you the safety to navigate the unknown, but allowing flexibility lets life surprise you. Don't be afraid to pivot, explore, or embrace the unexpected. Plans are important, but they're not everything. By balancing preparation with an openness to the unknown, you leave room for life's magic to unfold.

Trust the process and let yourself be amazed by what you discover.

What's Next?

Congratulations on completing this book filled with wisdom from real people! As you've journeyed through the pages, you've discovered the profound truth encapsulated in the quote:

Wisdom is the reward of experience and should be shared.

Your role as the bearer of this wisdom doesn't end here. Your journey is just beginning. Embrace the opportunity to continue sharing wisdom and to uplift and inspire others on their paths. Let this remind us that we should not hoard wisdom but generously share it with those in need.

So, my friend, as you close this book, carry its lessons forward. And remember, your experiences and life lessons are your wisdom. They are invaluable treasures waiting to be shared with the world. Let's continue to learn from one another, grow, and spread positive energy and wisdom wherever we go.

About the Author

Jen Fort is a writer, coach, and natural-born encourager who believes the right words at the right time can be a lifeline. She created the *Wisdom & Warnings* series to capture real advice from real people—because no one gets through life's biggest transitions without a little help. *Tips from the Quad* was born from the many mistakes, surprises, and lessons Jen experienced when her oldest went off to college. Jen's mission is to offer a steady, encouraging voice filled with honesty, heart, and a reminder that you're not in this alone.

Visit www.iamjenfort.com to:

- Share your favorite nuggets of wisdom and perhaps have your wisdom included in future books.
- Receive free resource suggestions.
- Be the first to know about upcoming Wisdom & Warnings book releases.
- Learn how you can benefit from Jen's mission to encourage and share life's lessons!

www.ingramcontent.com/pod-product-compliance
Lightning Source LLC
Chambersburg PA
CBHW060808120626
46557CB00001B/130